It's Your First Crush, Charlie Brown!

Charles M. Schulz

Ballantine Books • New York

A Ballantine Books Trade Paperback Original

Copyright © 2007 by United Feature Syndicate, Inc.

Published in the United States by Ballantine Books, an imprint of the
Random House Publishing Group, a division of Random House, Inc., New York.

BALLANTINE and colophon are registered trademarks of Random House, Inc.

The comic strips in this book were originally published in newspapers worldwide.

ISBN 978-0-345-47988-4

Printed in the United States of America

www.ballantinebooks.com

2 4 6 8 9 7 5 3 1

Book design by Diane Hobbing of Snap-Haus Graphics

It's Your First Crush, Charlie Brown!

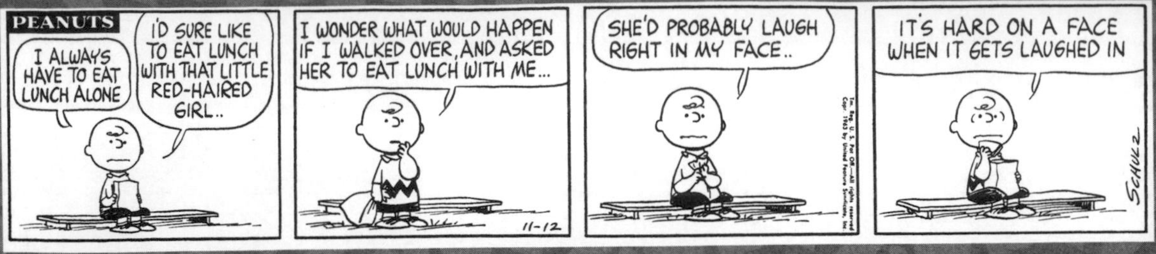
PEANUTS
I ALWAYS HAVE TO EAT LUNCH ALONE
I'D SURE LIKE TO EAT LUNCH WITH THAT LITTLE RED-HAIRED GIRL..
I WONDER WHAT WOULD HAPPEN IF I WALKED OVER, AND ASKED HER TO EAT LUNCH WITH ME...
11-12
SHE'D PROBABLY LAUGH RIGHT IN MY FACE..
Tm. Reg. U. S. Pat. Off.—All rights reserved
Copr. 1963 by United Feature Syndicate, Inc.
IT'S HARD ON A FACE WHEN IT GETS LAUGHED IN
SCHULZ

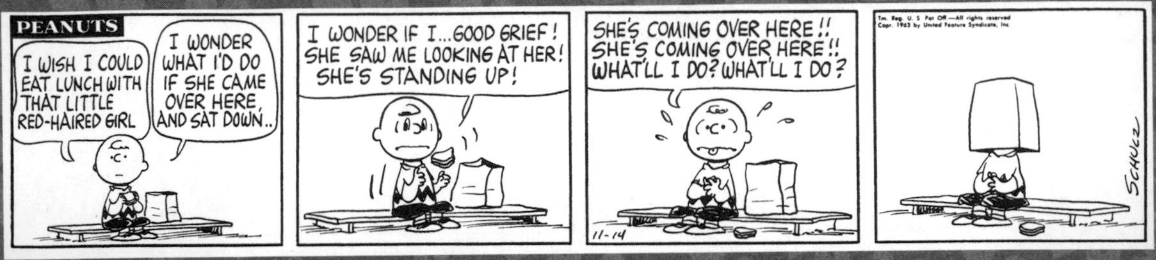
PEANUTS
I WISH I COULD EAT LUNCH WITH THAT LITTLE RED-HAIRED GIRL
I WONDER WHAT I'D DO IF SHE CAME OVER HERE AND SAT DOWN..
I WONDER IF I...GOOD GRIEF! SHE SAW ME LOOKING AT HER! SHE'S STANDING UP!
SHE'S COMING OVER HERE!! SHE'S COMING OVER HERE!! WHAT'LL I DO? WHAT'LL I DO?
11-14
Tm. Reg. U. S. Pat. Off.—All rights reserved
Copr. 1963 by United Feature Syndicate, Inc.
SCHULZ

PEANUTS
Tm. Reg. U. S. Pat. Off.—All rights reserved
Copr. 1963 by United Feature Syndicate, Inc.
SHE'S TALKING TO HIM..
11-16
THAT LITTLE RED-HAIRED GIRL IS TALKING TO HIM...AND NOW SHE'S GIVING HIM A BIG HUG!
I CAN'T STAND IT..
HOW DO **YOU** RATE?!
SCHULZ

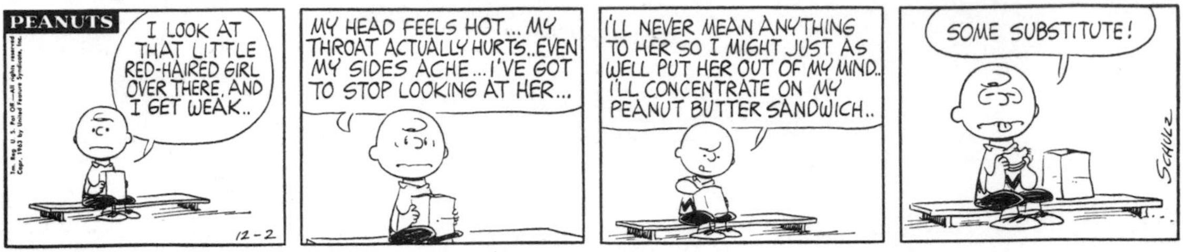
PEANUTS
I LOOK AT THAT LITTLE RED-HAIRED GIRL OVER THERE, AND I GET WEAK..
MY HEAD FEELS HOT... MY THROAT ACTUALLY HURTS..EVEN MY SIDES ACHE... I'VE GOT TO STOP LOOKING AT HER...
I'LL NEVER MEAN ANYTHING TO HER SO I MIGHT JUST AS WELL PUT HER OUT OF MY MIND.. I'LL CONCENTRATE ON MY PEANUT BUTTER SANDWICH..
SOME SUBSTITUTE!
12-2
SCHULZ

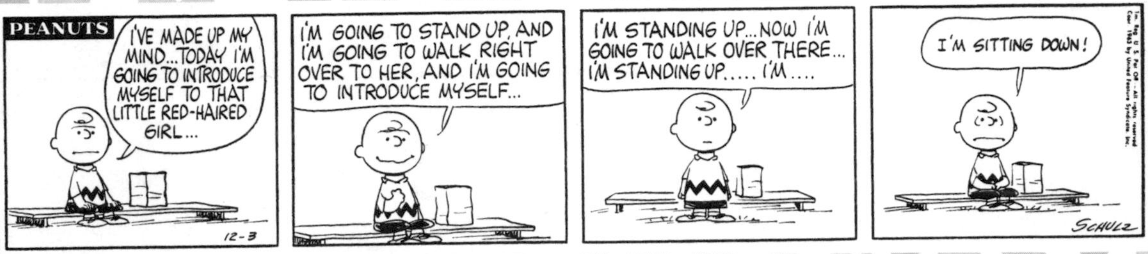
PEANUTS
I'VE MADE UP MY MIND...TODAY I'M GOING TO INTRODUCE MYSELF TO THAT LITTLE RED-HAIRED GIRL...
I'M GOING TO STAND UP, AND I'M GOING TO WALK RIGHT OVER TO HER, AND I'M GOING TO INTRODUCE MYSELF...
I'M STANDING UP...NOW I'M GOING TO WALK OVER THERE... I'M STANDING UP..... I'M....
I'M SITTING DOWN!
12-3
SCHULZ

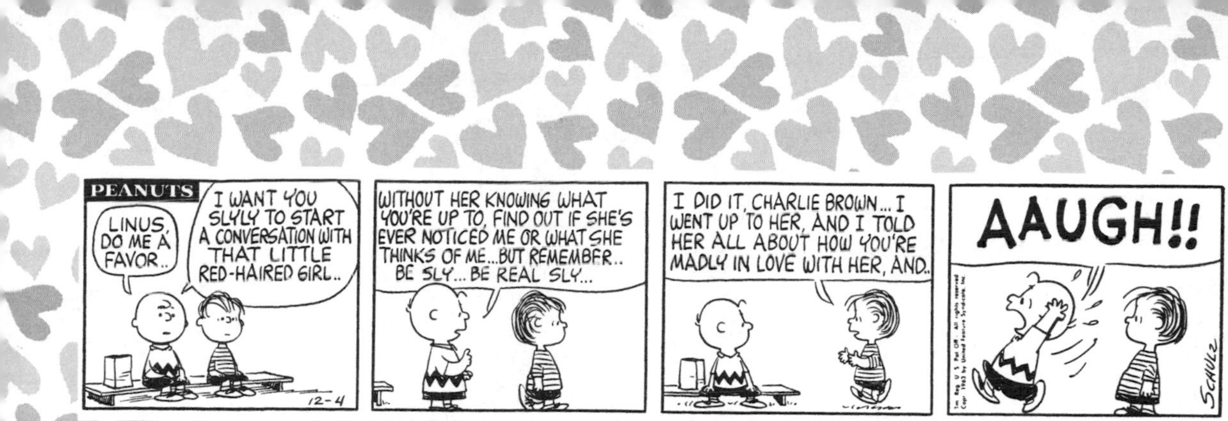
PEANUTS
LINUS, DO ME A FAVOR..
I WANT YOU SLYLY TO START A CONVERSATION WITH THAT LITTLE RED-HAIRED GIRL..
12-4
WITHOUT HER KNOWING WHAT YOU'RE UP TO, FIND OUT IF SHE'S EVER NOTICED ME OR WHAT SHE THINKS OF ME...BUT REMEMBER.. BE SLY... BE REAL SLY...
I DID IT, CHARLIE BROWN... I WENT UP TO HER, AND I TOLD HER ALL ABOUT HOW YOU'RE MADLY IN LOVE WITH HER, AND..
AAUGH!!
SCHULZ

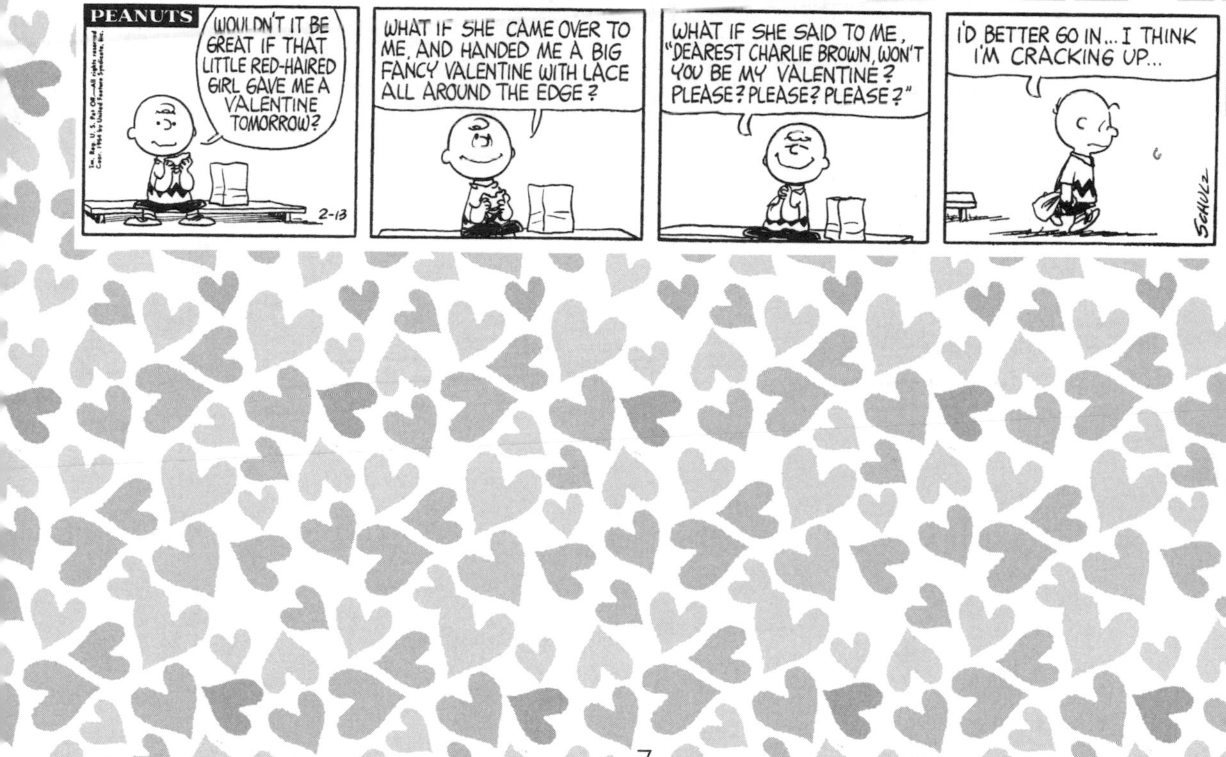
PEANUTS
WOULDN'T IT BE GREAT IF THAT LITTLE RED-HAIRED GIRL GAVE ME A VALENTINE TOMORROW?
2-13
WHAT IF SHE CAME OVER TO ME, AND HANDED ME A BIG FANCY VALENTINE WITH LACE ALL AROUND THE EDGE?
WHAT IF SHE SAID TO ME, "DEAREST CHARLIE BROWN, WON'T YOU BE MY VALENTINE? PLEASE? PLEASE? PLEASE?"
I'D BETTER GO IN... I THINK I'M CRACKING UP...
SCHULZ

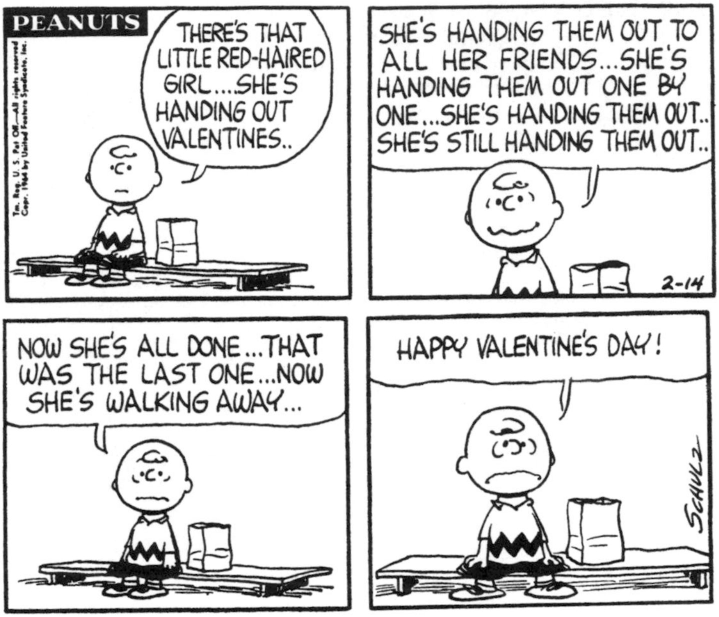
PEANUTS
Tm. Reg. U. S. Pat. Off.—All rights reserved
Copr. 1964 by United Feature Syndicate, Inc.
THERE'S THAT LITTLE RED-HAIRED GIRL....SHE'S HANDING OUT VALENTINES..
SHE'S HANDING THEM OUT TO ALL HER FRIENDS...SHE'S HANDING THEM OUT ONE BY ONE...SHE'S HANDING THEM OUT.. SHE'S STILL HANDING THEM OUT..
2-14
NOW SHE'S ALL DONE...THAT WAS THE LAST ONE...NOW SHE'S WALKING AWAY...
HAPPY VALENTINE'S DAY!
SCHULZ

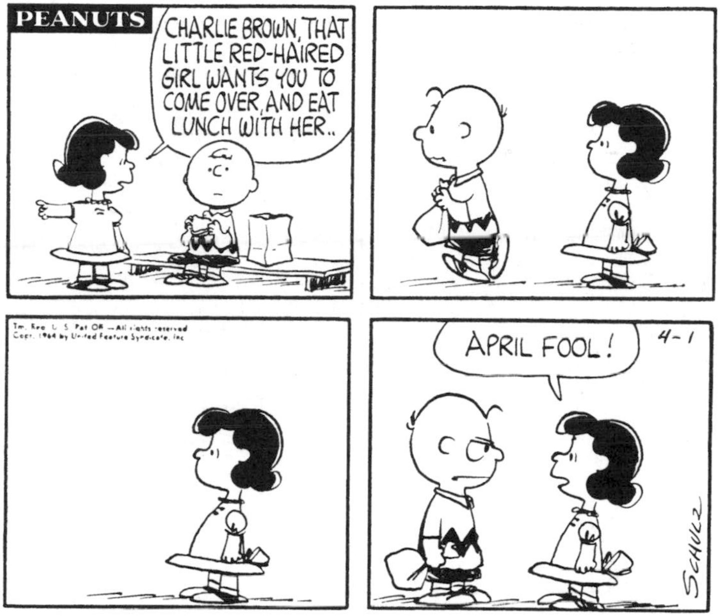
PEANUTS
CHARLIE BROWN, THAT LITTLE RED-HAIRED GIRL WANTS YOU TO COME OVER, AND EAT LUNCH WITH HER..
Tm. Reg. U. S. Pat. Off.—All rights reserved
Copr. 1964 by United Feature Syndicate, Inc
APRIL FOOL!
4-1
SCHULZ

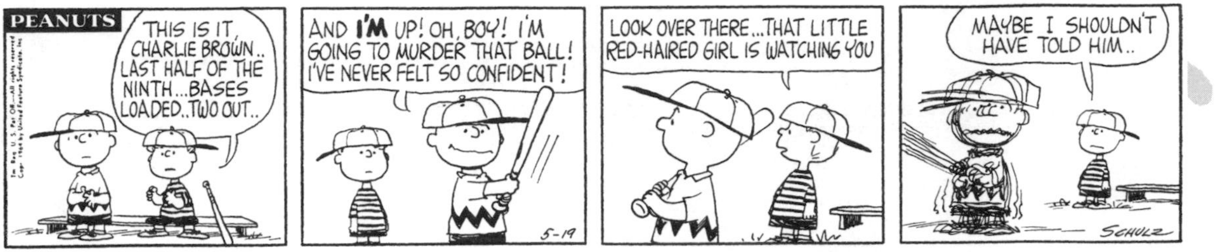
PEANUTS
THIS IS IT, CHARLIE BROWN.. LAST HALF OF THE NINTH...BASES LOADED..TWO OUT..
AND I'M UP! OH, BOY! I'M GOING TO MURDER THAT BALL! I'VE NEVER FELT SO CONFIDENT!
5-19
LOOK OVER THERE...THAT LITTLE RED-HAIRED GIRL IS WATCHING YOU
MAYBE I SHOULDN'T HAVE TOLD HIM..
SCHULZ

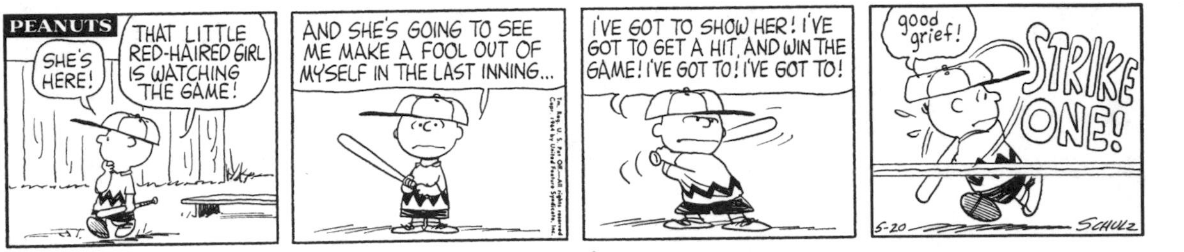
PEANUTS
SHE'S HERE!
THAT LITTLE RED-HAIRED GIRL IS WATCHING THE GAME!
AND SHE'S GOING TO SEE ME MAKE A FOOL OUT OF MYSELF IN THE LAST INNING...
I'VE GOT TO SHOW HER! I'VE GOT TO GET A HIT, AND WIN THE GAME! I'VE GOT TO! I'VE GOT TO!
good grief!
STRIKE ONE!
5-20
SCHULZ

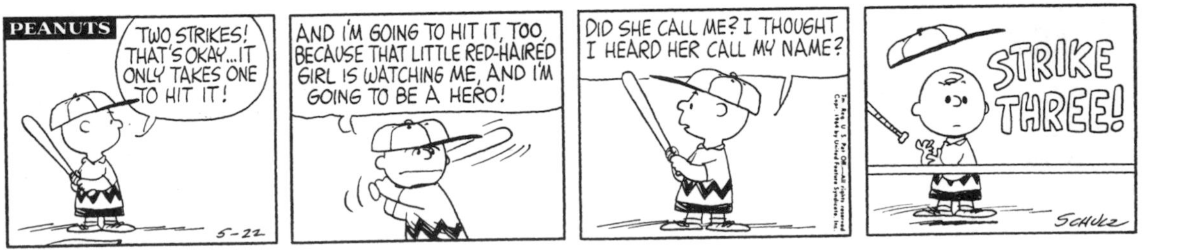
PEANUTS
TWO STRIKES! THAT'S OKAY...IT ONLY TAKES ONE TO HIT IT!
5-22
AND I'M GOING TO HIT IT, TOO, BECAUSE THAT LITTLE RED-HAIRED GIRL IS WATCHING ME, AND I'M GOING TO BE A HERO!
DID SHE CALL ME? I THOUGHT I HEARD HER CALL MY NAME?
STRIKE THREE!
SCHULZ

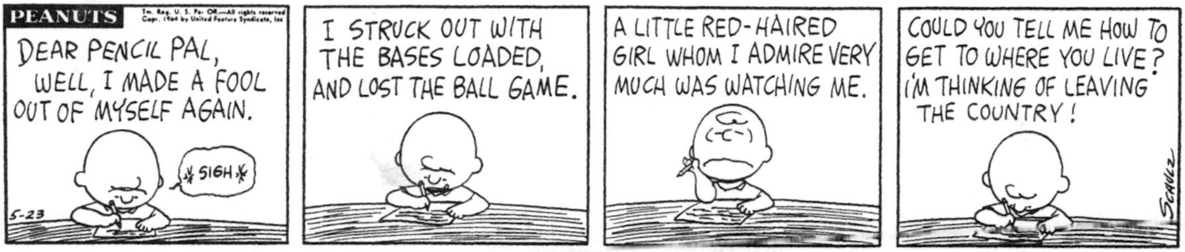
PEANUTS
Tm. Reg. U. S. Pat. Off.—All rights reserved
Copr. 1964 by United Feature Syndicate, Inc
DEAR PENCIL PAL,
WELL, I MADE A FOOL OUT OF MYSELF AGAIN.
SIGH
5-23
I STRUCK OUT WITH THE BASES LOADED, AND LOST THE BALL GAME.
A LITTLE RED-HAIRED GIRL WHOM I ADMIRE VERY MUCH WAS WATCHING ME.
COULD YOU TELL ME HOW TO GET TO WHERE YOU LIVE? I'M THINKING OF LEAVING THE COUNTRY!
SCHULZ

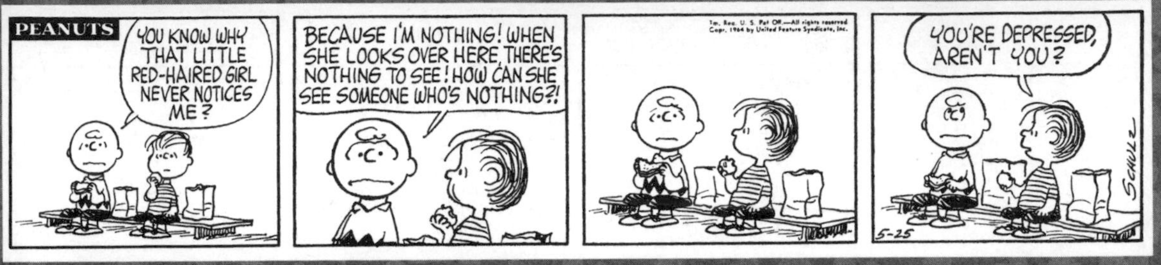
PEANUTS
YOU KNOW WHY THAT LITTLE RED-HAIRED GIRL NEVER NOTICES ME?
BECAUSE I'M NOTHING! WHEN SHE LOOKS OVER HERE, THERE'S NOTHING TO SEE! HOW CAN SHE SEE SOMEONE WHO'S NOTHING?!
Tm. Reg. U. S. Pat Off.—All rights reserved Copr. 1964 by United Feature Syndicate, Inc.
YOU'RE DEPRESSED, AREN'T YOU?
SCHULZ
5-25

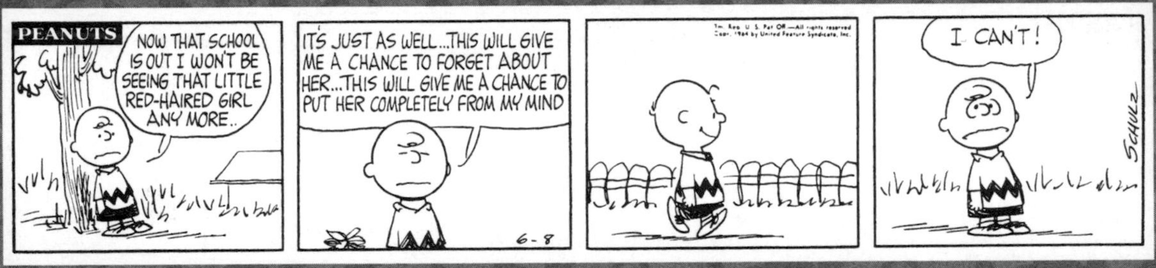
PEANUTS
NOW THAT SCHOOL IS OUT I WON'T BE SEEING THAT LITTLE RED-HAIRED GIRL ANY MORE..
IT'S JUST AS WELL...THIS WILL GIVE ME A CHANCE TO FORGET ABOUT HER...THIS WILL GIVE ME A CHANCE TO PUT HER COMPLETELY FROM MY MIND
6-8
Tm. Reg. U. S. Pat Off.—All rights reserved Copr. 1964 by United Feature Syndicate, Inc.
I CAN'T!
SCHULZ

PEANUTS
THAT LITTLE RED-HAIRED GIRL IS SURE CUTE..
I'D GIVE ANYTHING IN THE WORLD TO BE SITTING THERE NEXT TO HER EATING LUNCH..
12-15
BLEAH!
NOTHING TAKES THE TASTE OUT OF PEANUT BUTTER LIKE UNREQUITED LOVE!
SCHULZ

PEANUTS
WHY DON'T I GO OVER AND TALK TO THAT LITTLE RED-HAIRED GIRL?
I CAN'T... I JUST CAN'T...
I HATE MYSELF FOR NOT HAVING ENOUGH NERVE TO TALK TO HER!
12-17
WELL, THAT ISN'T EXACTLY TRUE...I HATE MYSELF FOR A LOT OF OTHER REASONS, TOO...
SCHULZ

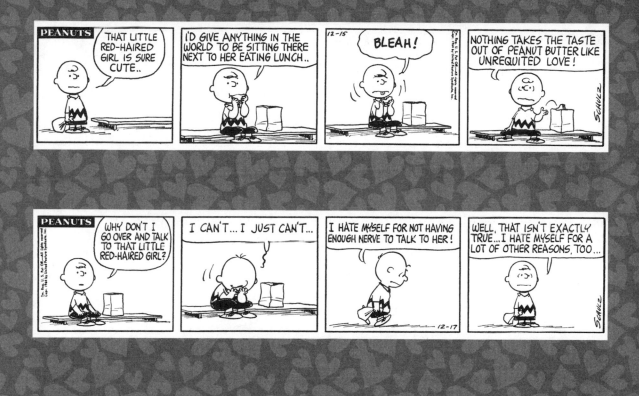

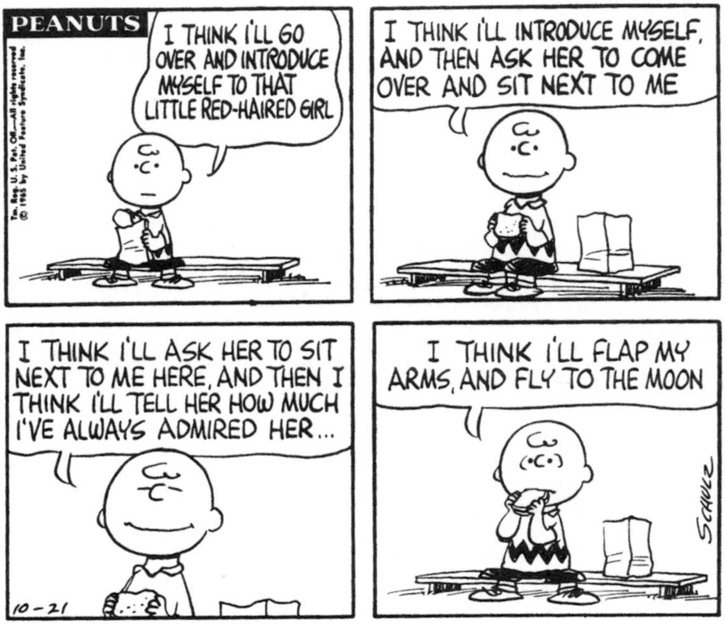
PEANUTS
Tm. Reg. U. S. Pat. Off.—All rights reserved © 1965 by United Feature Syndicate, Inc.
I THINK I'LL GO OVER AND INTRODUCE MYSELF TO THAT LITTLE RED-HAIRED GIRL
I THINK I'LL INTRODUCE MYSELF, AND THEN ASK HER TO COME OVER AND SIT NEXT TO ME
I THINK I'LL ASK HER TO SIT NEXT TO ME HERE, AND THEN I THINK I'LL TELL HER HOW MUCH I'VE ALWAYS ADMIRED HER...
10-21
I THINK I'LL FLAP MY ARMS, AND FLY TO THE MOON
SCHULZ

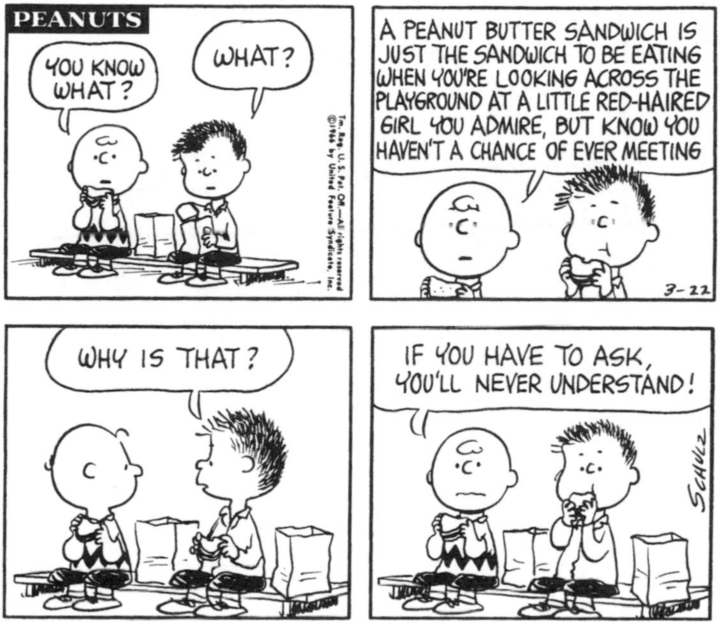
PEANUTS
YOU KNOW WHAT?
WHAT?
Tm. Reg. U. S. Pat. Off.—All rights reserved
©1966 by United Feature Syndicate, Inc.
A PEANUT BUTTER SANDWICH IS JUST THE SANDWICH TO BE EATING WHEN YOU'RE LOOKING ACROSS THE PLAYGROUND AT A LITTLE RED-HAIRED GIRL YOU ADMIRE, BUT KNOW YOU HAVEN'T A CHANCE OF EVER MEETING
3-22
WHY IS THAT?
IF YOU HAVE TO ASK, YOU'LL NEVER UNDERSTAND!
SCHULZ

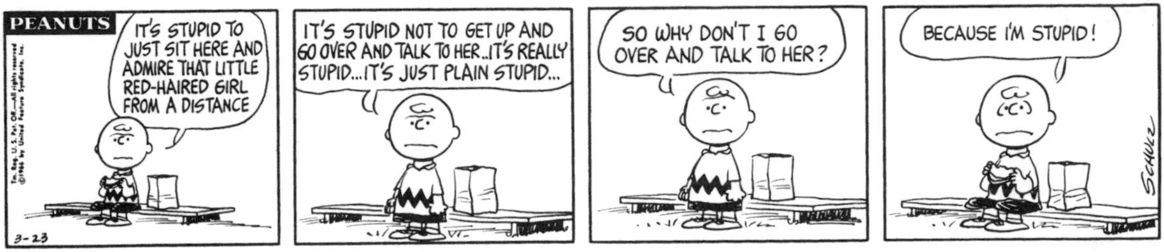
PEANUTS
Tm. Reg. U. S. Pat. Off.—All rights reserved
©1966 by United Feature Syndicate, Inc.
3-23
IT'S STUPID TO JUST SIT HERE AND ADMIRE THAT LITTLE RED-HAIRED GIRL FROM A DISTANCE
IT'S STUPID NOT TO GET UP AND GO OVER AND TALK TO HER..IT'S REALLY STUPID...IT'S JUST PLAIN STUPID...
SO WHY DON'T I GO OVER AND TALK TO HER?
BECAUSE I'M STUPID!
SCHULZ

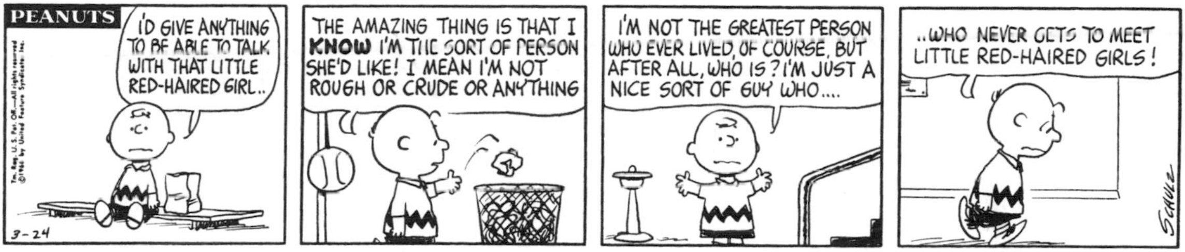
PEANUTS
I'D GIVE ANYTHING TO BE ABLE TO TALK WITH THAT LITTLE RED-HAIRED GIRL..
Tm. Reg. U. S. Pat. Off.—All rights reserved
3-24
THE AMAZING THING IS THAT I **KNOW** I'M THE SORT OF PERSON SHE'D LIKE! I MEAN I'M NOT ROUGH OR CRUDE OR ANYTHING
I'M NOT THE GREATEST PERSON WHO EVER LIVED, OF COURSE, BUT AFTER ALL, WHO IS? I'M JUST A NICE SORT OF GUY WHO....
..WHO NEVER GETS TO MEET LITTLE RED-HAIRED GIRLS!
SCHULZ

PEANUTS
WHAT'S THIS? THAT LITTLE RED-HAIRED GIRL DROPPED HER PENCIL...
GEE... IT'S GOT TEETH MARKS ALL OVER IT...
SHE NIBBLES ON HER PENCIL...
SHE'S HUMAN!
SCHULZ
3-25

PEANUTS
WHAT'S THAT YOU'RE HOLDING?
3-26
IT'S A PENCIL... IT BELONGS TO THAT LITTLE RED-HAIRED GIRL... I'M GOING TO STAND HERE UNTIL SHE WALKS BY, AND THEN I'M GOING TO TELL HER HOW I FOUND IT...
I HATE TO SEE YOU GO TO ALL THAT TROUBLE, CHARLIE BROWN... WHY DON'T I JUST GIVE IT TO HER?
HEY! HERE'S YOUR STUPID PENCIL!!
SCHULZ

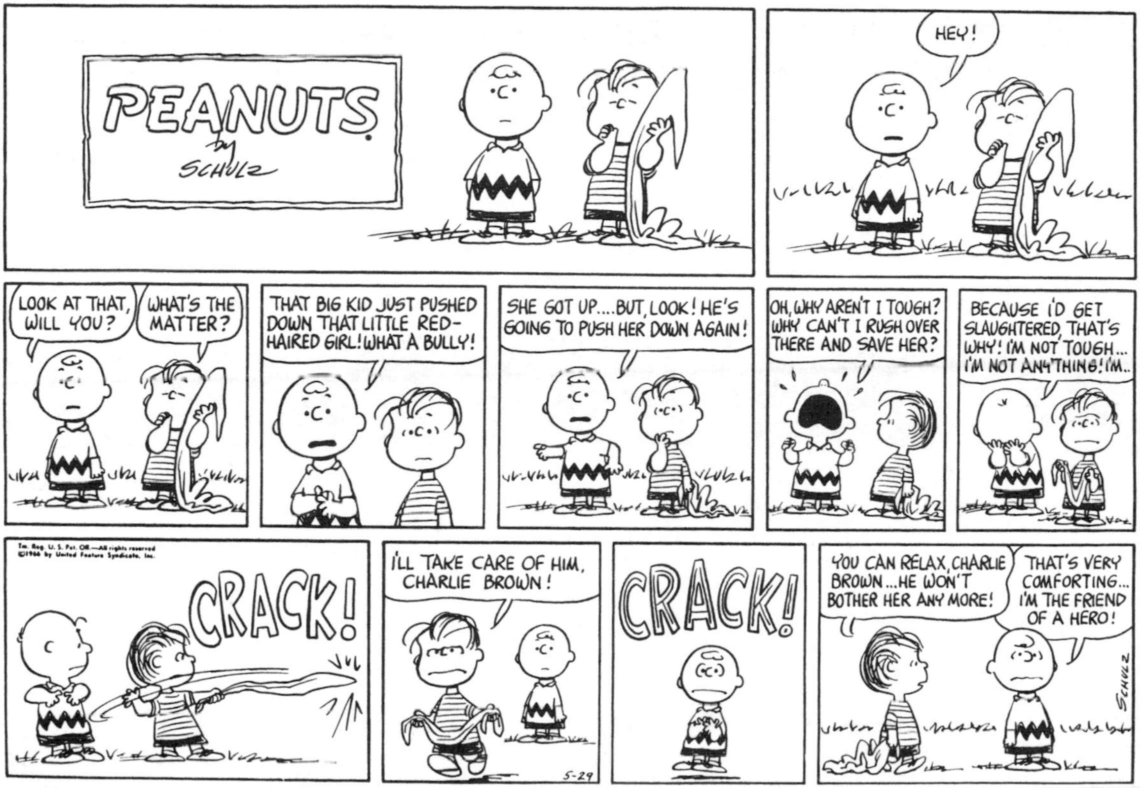
PEANUTS
by SCHULZ
HEY!
LOOK AT THAT, WILL YOU?
WHAT'S THE MATTER?
THAT BIG KID JUST PUSHED DOWN THAT LITTLE RED-HAIRED GIRL! WHAT A BULLY!
SHE GOT UP....BUT, LOOK! HE'S GOING TO PUSH HER DOWN AGAIN!
OH, WHY AREN'T I TOUGH? WHY CAN'T I RUSH OVER THERE AND SAVE HER?
BECAUSE I'D GET SLAUGHTERED, THAT'S WHY! I'M NOT TOUGH... I'M NOT ANYTHING! I'M..
Tm. Reg. U. S. Pat. Off.—All rights reserved
©1966 by United Feature Syndicate, Inc.
CRACK!
I'LL TAKE CARE OF HIM, CHARLIE BROWN!
5-29
CRACK!
YOU CAN RELAX, CHARLIE BROWN...HE WON'T BOTHER HER ANY MORE!
THAT'S VERY COMFORTING... I'M THE FRIEND OF A HERO!
SCHULZ

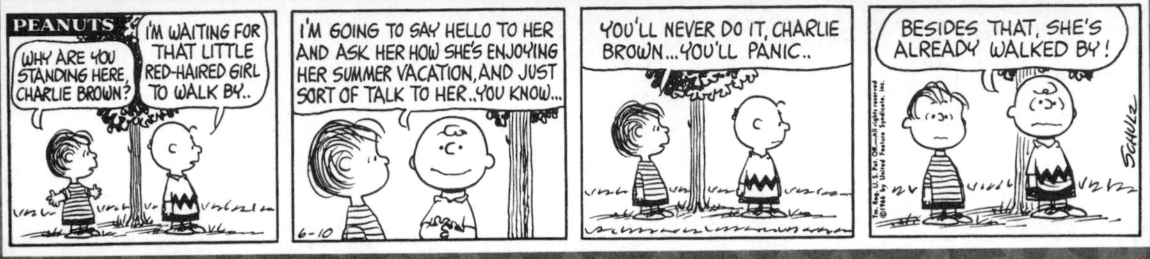
PEANUTS
WHY ARE YOU STANDING HERE, CHARLIE BROWN?
I'M WAITING FOR THAT LITTLE RED-HAIRED GIRL TO WALK BY..
I'M GOING TO SAY HELLO TO HER AND ASK HER HOW SHE'S ENJOYING HER SUMMER VACATION, AND JUST SORT OF TALK TO HER..YOU KNOW...
6-10
YOU'LL NEVER DO IT, CHARLIE BROWN...YOU'LL PANIC..
BESIDES THAT, SHE'S ALREADY WALKED BY!
SCHULZ

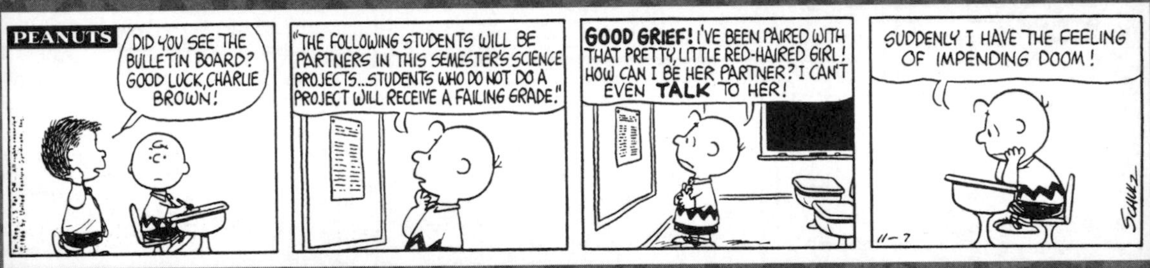
PEANUTS
DID YOU SEE THE BULLETIN BOARD? GOOD LUCK, CHARLIE BROWN!
"THE FOLLOWING STUDENTS WILL BE PARTNERS IN THIS SEMESTER'S SCIENCE PROJECTS...STUDENTS WHO DO NOT DO A PROJECT WILL RECEIVE A FAILING GRADE."
GOOD GRIEF! I'VE BEEN PAIRED WITH THAT PRETTY, LITTLE RED-HAIRED GIRL! HOW CAN I BE HER PARTNER? I CAN'T EVEN TALK TO HER!
SUDDENLY I HAVE THE FEELING OF IMPENDING DOOM!
11-7
SCHULZ

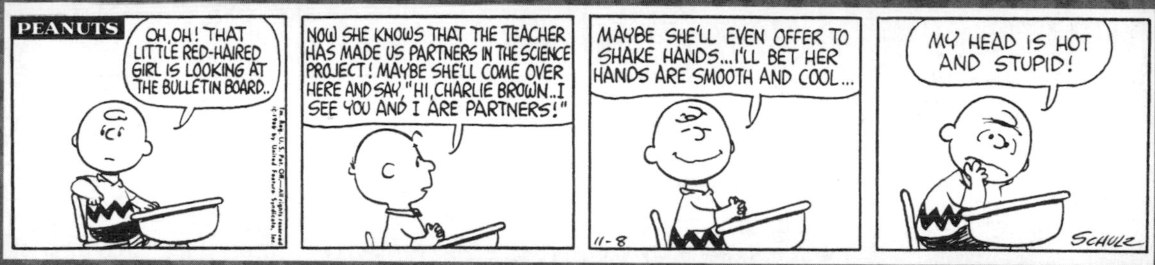
PEANUTS
OH, OH! THAT LITTLE RED-HAIRED GIRL IS LOOKING AT THE BULLETIN BOARD..
NOW SHE KNOWS THAT THE TEACHER HAS MADE US PARTNERS IN THE SCIENCE PROJECT! MAYBE SHE'LL COME OVER HERE AND SAY, "HI, CHARLIE BROWN..I SEE YOU AND I ARE PARTNERS!"
MAYBE SHE'LL EVEN OFFER TO SHAKE HANDS...I'LL BET HER HANDS ARE SMOOTH AND COOL...
11-8
MY HEAD IS HOT AND STUPID!
SCHULZ

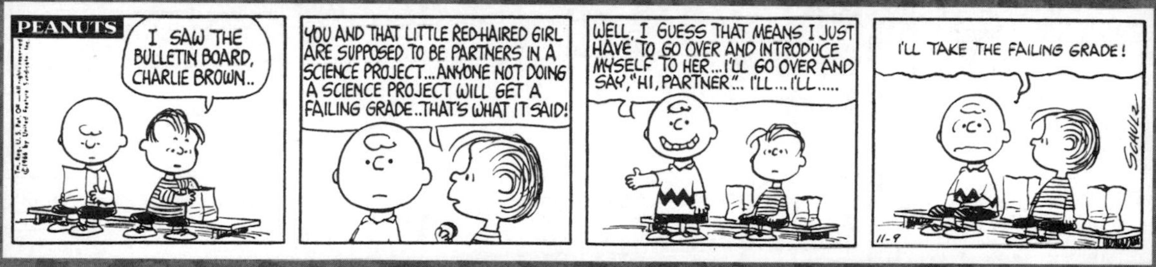
PEANUTS
I SAW THE BULLETIN BOARD, CHARLIE BROWN..
YOU AND THAT LITTLE RED-HAIRED GIRL ARE SUPPOSED TO BE PARTNERS IN A SCIENCE PROJECT...ANYONE NOT DOING A SCIENCE PROJECT WILL GET A FAILING GRADE..THAT'S WHAT IT SAID!
WELL, I GUESS THAT MEANS I JUST HAVE TO GO OVER AND INTRODUCE MYSELF TO HER...I'LL GO OVER AND SAY, "HI, PARTNER"... I'LL... I'LL.....
I'LL TAKE THE FAILING GRADE!
SCHULZ
11-9

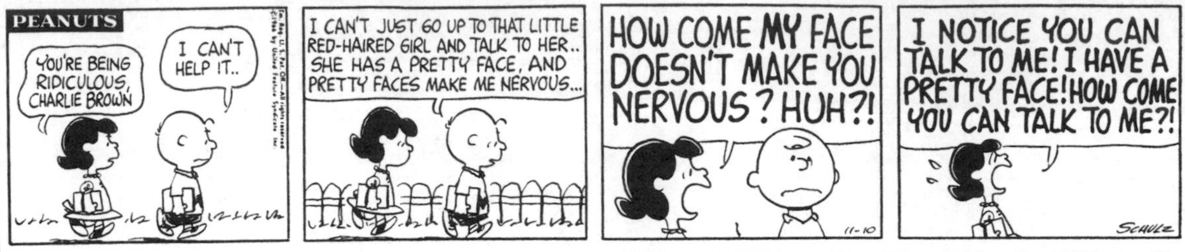
PEANUTS
YOU'RE BEING RIDICULOUS, CHARLIE BROWN
I CAN'T HELP IT..
I CAN'T JUST GO UP TO THAT LITTLE RED-HAIRED GIRL AND TALK TO HER.. SHE HAS A PRETTY FACE, AND PRETTY FACES MAKE ME NERVOUS...
HOW COME MY FACE DOESN'T MAKE YOU NERVOUS? HUH?!
11-10
I NOTICE YOU CAN TALK TO ME! I HAVE A PRETTY FACE! HOW COME YOU CAN TALK TO ME?!
SCHULZ

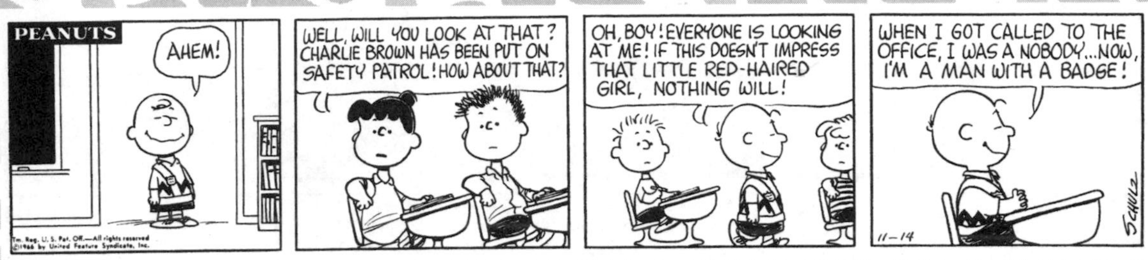
PEANUTS
AHEM!
WELL, WILL YOU LOOK AT THAT? CHARLIE BROWN HAS BEEN PUT ON SAFETY PATROL! HOW ABOUT THAT?
OH, BOY! EVERYONE IS LOOKING AT ME! IF THIS DOESN'T IMPRESS THAT LITTLE RED-HAIRED GIRL, NOTHING WILL!
WHEN I GOT CALLED TO THE OFFICE, I WAS A NOBODY...NOW, I'M A MAN WITH A BADGE!
11-14
SCHULZ

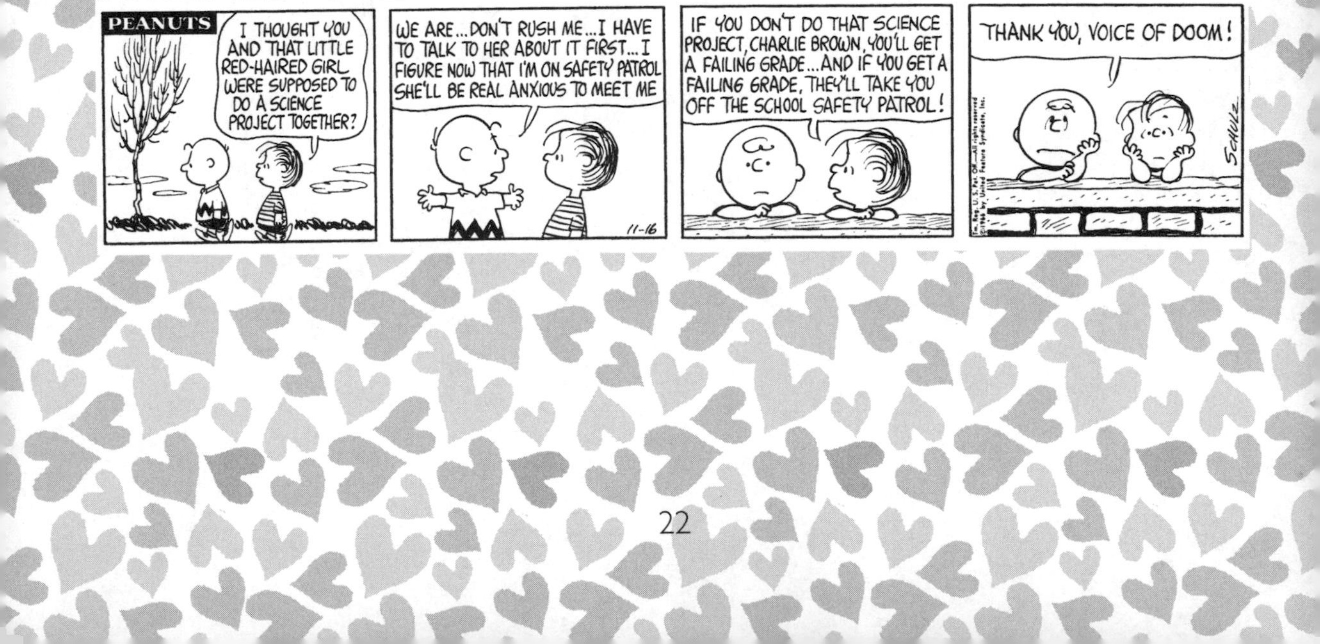
PEANUTS
I THOUGHT YOU AND THAT LITTLE RED-HAIRED GIRL WERE SUPPOSED TO DO A SCIENCE PROJECT TOGETHER?
WE ARE...DON'T RUSH ME...I HAVE TO TALK TO HER ABOUT IT FIRST...I FIGURE NOW THAT I'M ON SAFETY PATROL SHE'LL BE REAL ANXIOUS TO MEET ME
11-16
IF YOU DON'T DO THAT SCIENCE PROJECT, CHARLIE BROWN, YOU'LL GET A FAILING GRADE...AND IF YOU GET A FAILING GRADE, THEY'LL TAKE YOU OFF THE SCHOOL SAFETY PATROL!
THANK YOU, VOICE OF DOOM!
SCHULZ

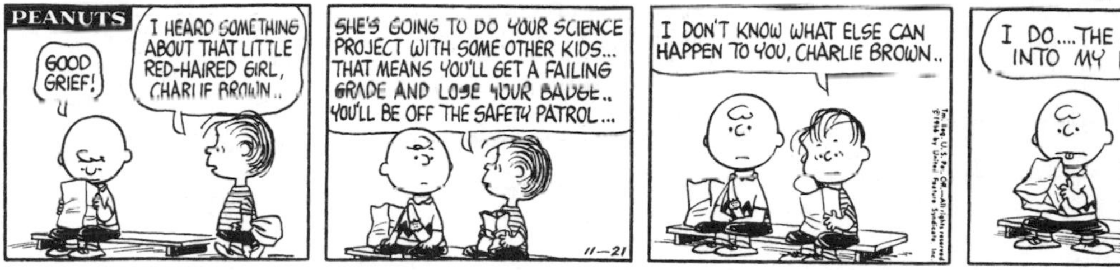
PEANUTS
GOOD GRIEF!
I HEARD SOMETHING ABOUT THAT LITTLE RED-HAIRED GIRL, CHARLIE BROWN..
SHE'S GOING TO DO YOUR SCIENCE PROJECT WITH SOME OTHER KIDS... THAT MEANS YOU'LL GET A FAILING GRADE AND LOSE YOUR BADGE.. YOU'LL BE OFF THE SAFETY PATROL...
11-21
I DON'T KNOW WHAT ELSE CAN HAPPEN TO YOU, CHARLIE BROWN..
I DO....THE ANTS GOT INTO MY LUNCH!
SCHULZ

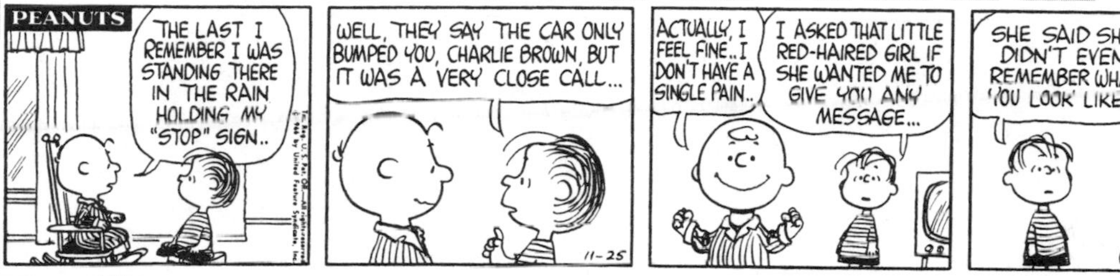
PEANUTS
THE LAST I REMEMBER I WAS STANDING THERE IN THE RAIN HOLDING MY "STOP" SIGN..
WELL, THEY SAY THE CAR ONLY BUMPED YOU, CHARLIE BROWN, BUT IT WAS A VERY CLOSE CALL...
11-25
ACTUALLY, I FEEL FINE..I DON'T HAVE A SINGLE PAIN..
I ASKED THAT LITTLE RED-HAIRED GIRL IF SHE WANTED ME TO GIVE YOU ANY MESSAGE...
SHE SAID SHE DIDN'T EVEN REMEMBER WHAT YOU LOOK LIKE!
I HURT ALL OVER!
SCHULZ

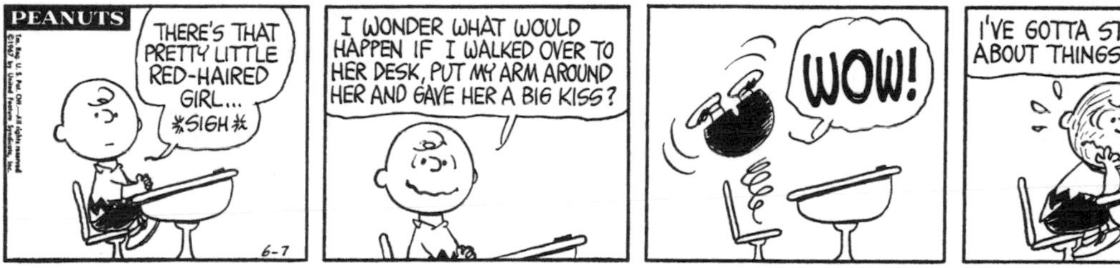
PEANUTS
THERE'S THAT PRETTY LITTLE RED-HAIRED GIRL... *SIGH*
6-7
I WONDER WHAT WOULD HAPPEN IF I WALKED OVER TO HER DESK, PUT MY ARM AROUND HER AND GAVE HER A BIG KISS?
WOW!
I'VE GOTTA STOP THINKING ABOUT THINGS LIKE THAT!
SCHULZ

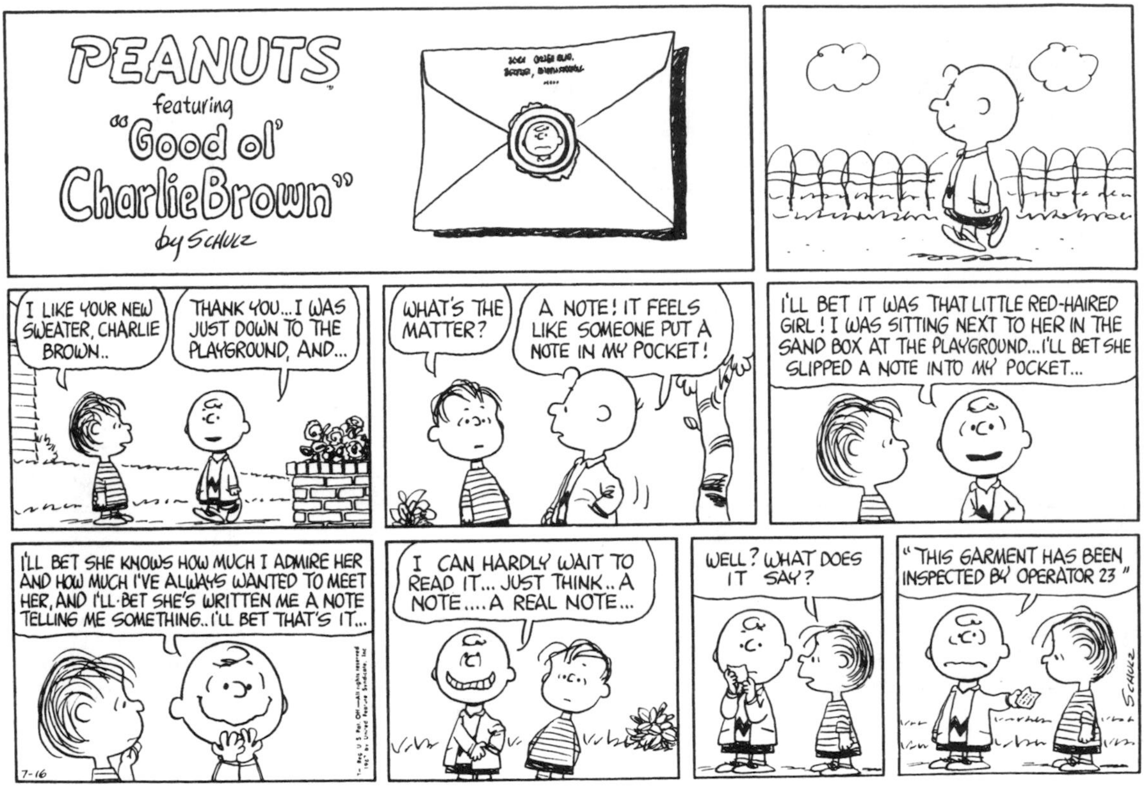
PEANUTS
featuring
"Good ol' CharlieBrown"
by SCHULZ
I LIKE YOUR NEW SWEATER, CHARLIE BROWN..
THANK YOU...I WAS JUST DOWN TO THE PLAYGROUND, AND...
WHAT'S THE MATTER?
A NOTE! IT FEELS LIKE SOMEONE PUT A NOTE IN MY POCKET!
I'LL BET IT WAS THAT LITTLE RED-HAIRED GIRL! I WAS SITTING NEXT TO HER IN THE SAND BOX AT THE PLAYGROUND...I'LL BET SHE SLIPPED A NOTE INTO MY POCKET...
I'LL BET SHE KNOWS HOW MUCH I ADMIRE HER AND HOW MUCH I'VE ALWAYS WANTED TO MEET HER, AND I'LL BET SHE'S WRITTEN ME A NOTE TELLING ME SOMETHING..I'LL BET THAT'S IT...
7-16
I CAN HARDLY WAIT TO READ IT... JUST THINK..A NOTE....A REAL NOTE...
WELL? WHAT DOES IT SAY?
"THIS GARMENT HAS BEEN INSPECTED BY OPERATOR 23"
SCHULZ

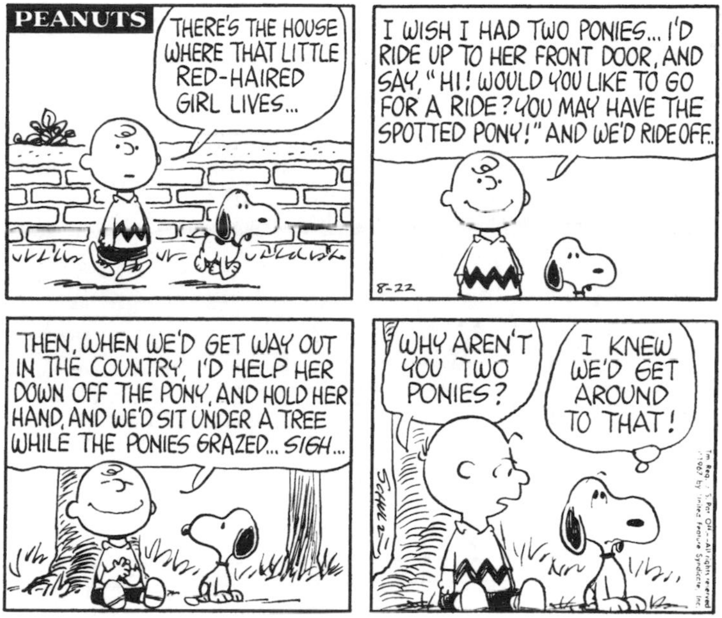
PEANUTS
THERE'S THE HOUSE WHERE THAT LITTLE RED-HAIRED GIRL LIVES...
I WISH I HAD TWO PONIES... I'D RIDE UP TO HER FRONT DOOR, AND SAY, "HI! WOULD YOU LIKE TO GO FOR A RIDE? YOU MAY HAVE THE SPOTTED PONY!" AND WE'D RIDE OFF...
8-22
THEN, WHEN WE'D GET WAY OUT IN THE COUNTRY, I'D HELP HER DOWN OFF THE PONY, AND HOLD HER HAND, AND WE'D SIT UNDER A TREE WHILE THE PONIES GRAZED... SIGH...
WHY AREN'T YOU TWO PONIES?
I KNEW WE'D GET AROUND TO THAT!
SCHULZ

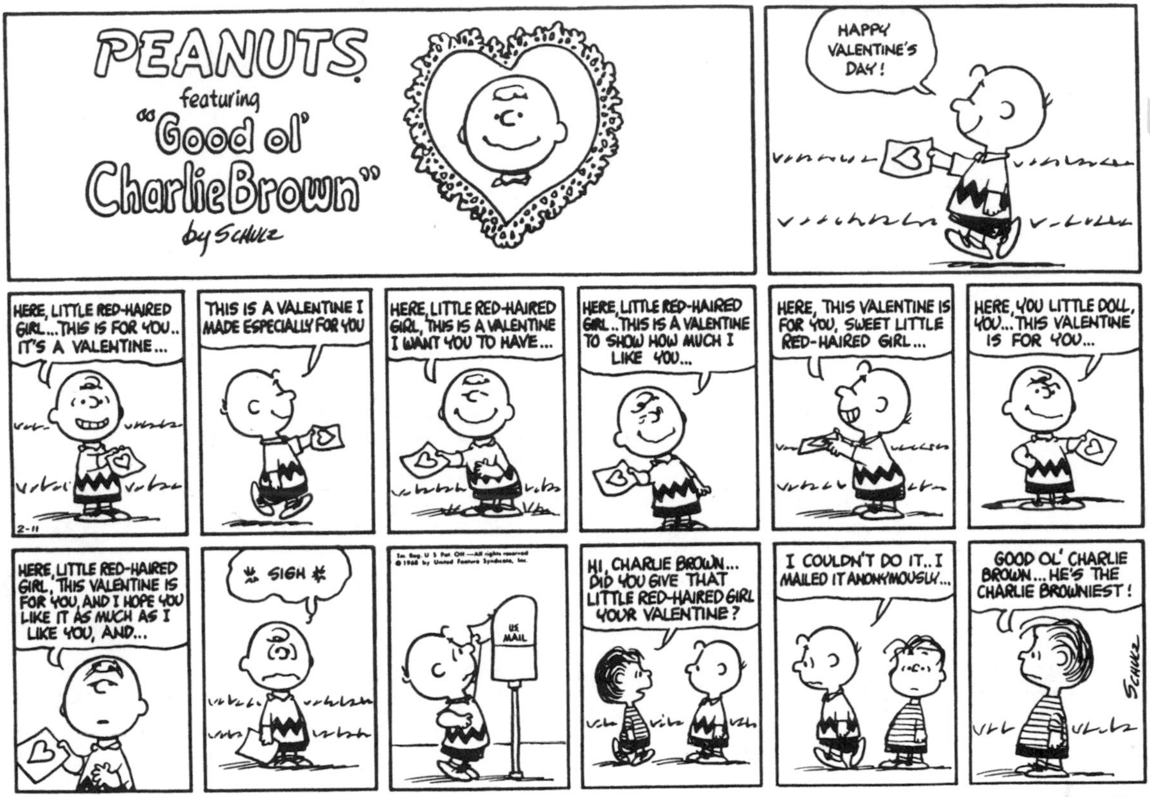
PEANUTS
featuring
"Good ol' Charlie Brown"
by SCHULZ
HAPPY VALENTINE'S DAY!
HERE, LITTLE RED-HAIRED GIRL...THIS IS FOR YOU.. IT'S A VALENTINE...
2-11
THIS IS A VALENTINE I MADE ESPECIALLY FOR YOU
HERE, LITTLE RED-HAIRED GIRL, THIS IS A VALENTINE I WANT YOU TO HAVE...
HERE, LITTLE RED-HAIRED GIRL..THIS IS A VALENTINE TO SHOW HOW MUCH I LIKE YOU...
HERE, THIS VALENTINE IS FOR YOU, SWEET LITTLE RED-HAIRED GIRL...
HERE, YOU LITTLE DOLL, YOU...THIS VALENTINE IS FOR YOU...
HERE, LITTLE RED-HAIRED GIRL, THIS VALENTINE IS FOR YOU, AND I HOPE YOU LIKE IT AS MUCH AS I LIKE YOU, AND...
SIGH
Tm. Reg. U S Pat. Off.—All rights reserved
© 1968 by United Feature Syndicate, Inc.
U.S. MAIL
HI, CHARLIE BROWN... DID YOU GIVE THAT LITTLE RED-HAIRED GIRL YOUR VALENTINE?
I COULDN'T DO IT.. I MAILED IT ANONYMOUSLY...
GOOD OL' CHARLIE BROWN... HE'S THE CHARLIE BROWNIEST!
SCHULZ

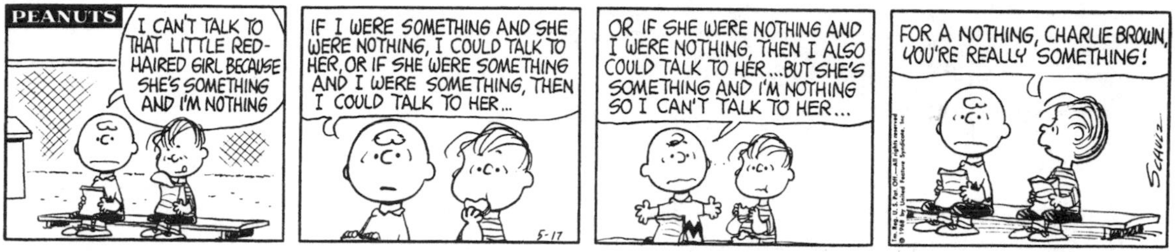
PEANUTS
I CAN'T TALK TO THAT LITTLE RED-HAIRED GIRL BECAUSE SHE'S SOMETHING AND I'M NOTHING
IF I WERE SOMETHING AND SHE WERE NOTHING, I COULD TALK TO HER, OR IF SHE WERE SOMETHING AND I WERE SOMETHING, THEN I COULD TALK TO HER...
5-17
OR IF SHE WERE NOTHING AND I WERE NOTHING, THEN I ALSO COULD TALK TO HER...BUT SHE'S SOMETHING AND I'M NOTHING SO I CAN'T TALK TO HER...
Tm. Reg. U. S. Pat. Off.—All rights reserved © 1968 by United Feature Syndicate, Inc.
FOR A NOTHING, CHARLIE BROWN, YOU'RE REALLY SOMETHING!
SCHULZ

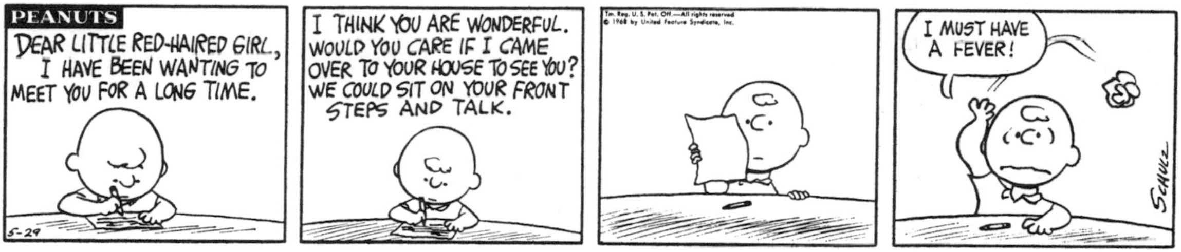
PEANUTS
DEAR LITTLE RED-HAIRED GIRL, I HAVE BEEN WANTING TO MEET YOU FOR A LONG TIME.
5-29
I THINK YOU ARE WONDERFUL. WOULD YOU CARE IF I CAME OVER TO YOUR HOUSE TO SEE YOU? WE COULD SIT ON YOUR FRONT STEPS AND TALK.
Tm. Reg. U. S. Pat. Off.—All rights reserved © 1968 by United Feature Syndicate, Inc.
I MUST HAVE A FEVER!
SCHULZ

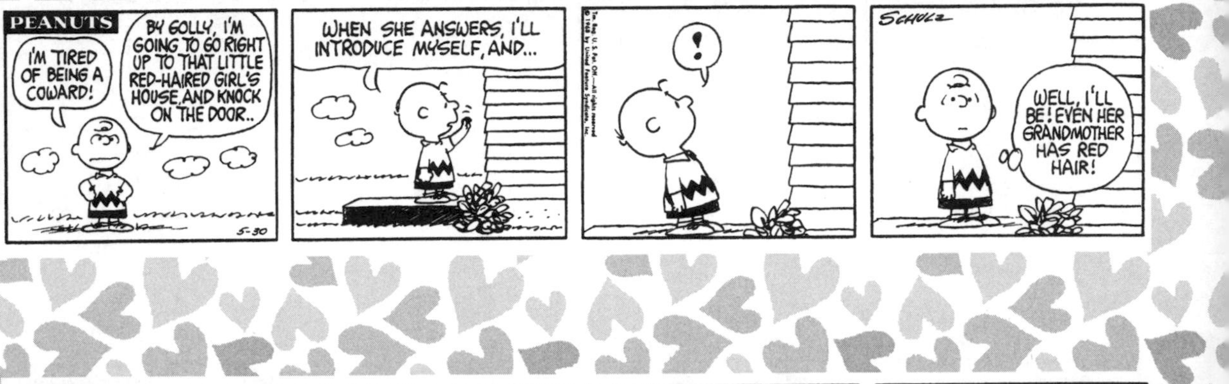
PEANUTS
I'M TIRED OF BEING A COWARD!
BY GOLLY, I'M GOING TO GO RIGHT UP TO THAT LITTLE RED-HAIRED GIRL'S HOUSE, AND KNOCK ON THE DOOR..
5-30
WHEN SHE ANSWERS, I'LL INTRODUCE MYSELF, AND...
!
SCHULZ
WELL, I'LL BE! EVEN HER GRANDMOTHER HAS RED HAIR!

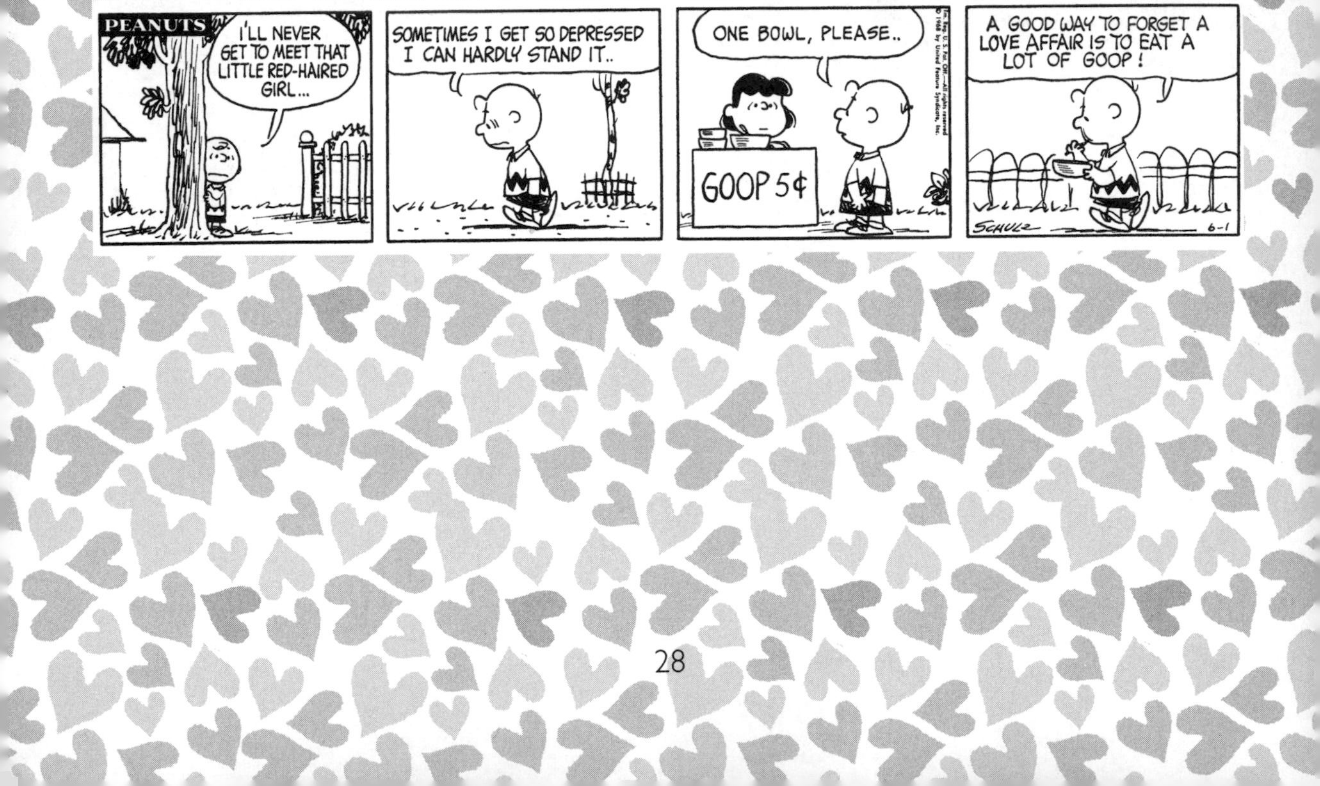
PEANUTS
I'LL NEVER GET TO MEET THAT LITTLE RED-HAIRED GIRL...
SOMETIMES I GET SO DEPRESSED I CAN HARDLY STAND IT..
ONE BOWL, PLEASE..
GOOP 5¢
A GOOD WAY TO FORGET A LOVE AFFAIR IS TO EAT A LOT OF GOOP!
SCHULZ
6-1

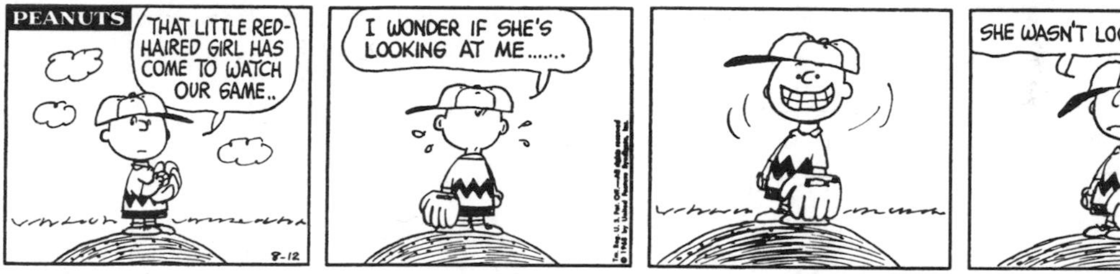
PEANUTS
THAT LITTLE RED-HAIRED GIRL HAS COME TO WATCH OUR GAME..
8-12
I WONDER IF SHE'S LOOKING AT ME.......
SHE WASN'T LOOKING AT ME...
SCHULZ

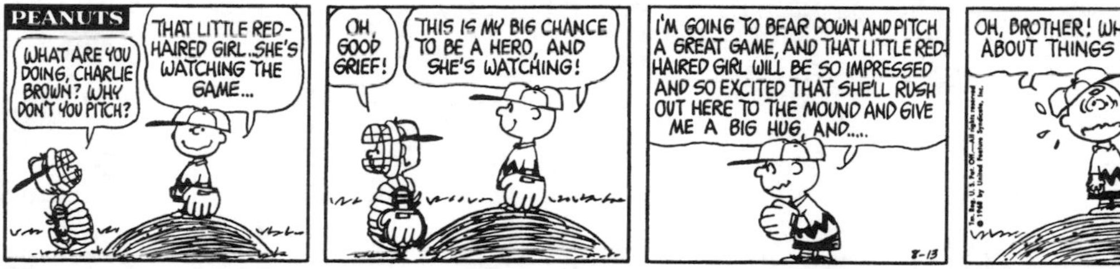
PEANUTS
WHAT ARE YOU DOING, CHARLIE BROWN? WHY DON'T YOU PITCH?
THAT LITTLE RED-HAIRED GIRL..SHE'S WATCHING THE GAME...
OH, GOOD GRIEF!
THIS IS MY BIG CHANCE TO BE A HERO, AND SHE'S WATCHING!
I'M GOING TO BEAR DOWN AND PITCH A GREAT GAME, AND THAT LITTLE RED-HAIRED GIRL WILL BE SO IMPRESSED AND SO EXCITED THAT SHE'LL RUSH OUT HERE TO THE MOUND AND GIVE ME A BIG HUG, AND....
8-13
OH, BROTHER! WHY DO I THINK ABOUT THINGS LIKE THAT?
SCHULZ

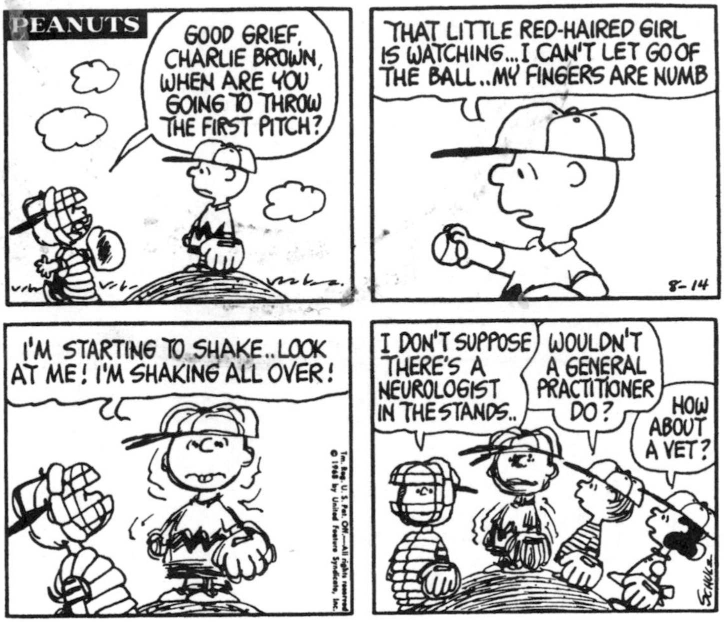
PEANUTS
GOOD GRIEF, CHARLIE BROWN, WHEN ARE YOU GOING TO THROW THE FIRST PITCH?
THAT LITTLE RED-HAIRED GIRL IS WATCHING...I CAN'T LET GO OF THE BALL..MY FINGERS ARE NUMB
8-14
I'M STARTING TO SHAKE..LOOK AT ME! I'M SHAKING ALL OVER!
Tm. Reg. U. S. Pat. Off.—All rights reserved © 1968 by United Feature Syndicate, Inc.
I DON'T SUPPOSE THERE'S A NEUROLOGIST IN THE STANDS..
WOULDN'T A GENERAL PRACTITIONER DO?
HOW ABOUT A VET?
SCHULZ

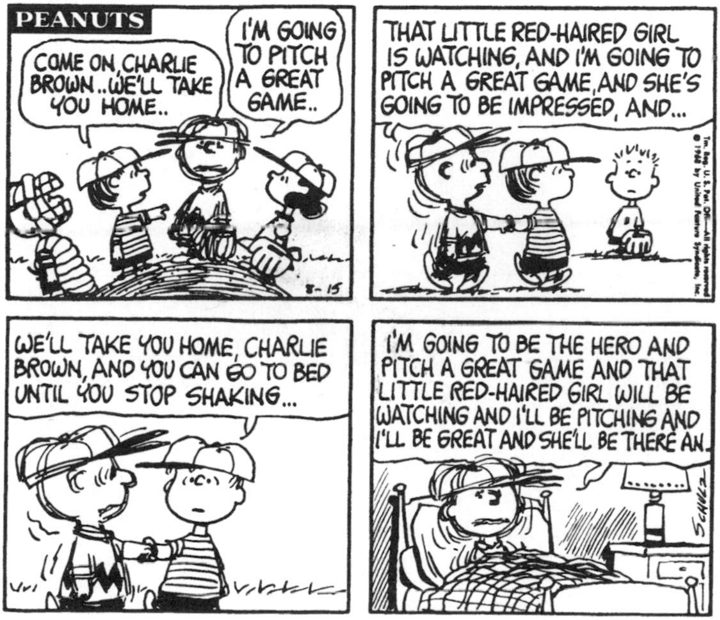
PEANUTS
COME ON, CHARLIE BROWN..WE'LL TAKE YOU HOME..
I'M GOING TO PITCH A GREAT GAME..
8-15
THAT LITTLE RED-HAIRED GIRL IS WATCHING, AND I'M GOING TO PITCH A GREAT GAME, AND SHE'S GOING TO BE IMPRESSED, AND...
WE'LL TAKE YOU HOME, CHARLIE BROWN, AND YOU CAN GO TO BED UNTIL YOU STOP SHAKING...
I'M GOING TO BE THE HERO AND PITCH A GREAT GAME AND THAT LITTLE RED-HAIRED GIRL WILL BE WATCHING AND I'LL BE PITCHING AND I'LL BE GREAT AND SHE'LL BE THERE AN..
SCHULZ

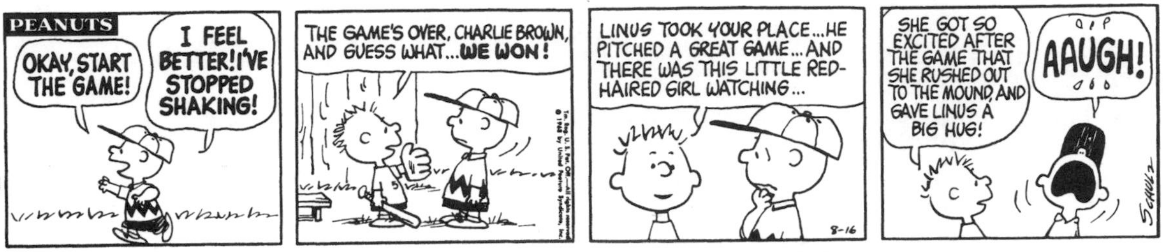
PEANUTS
OKAY, START THE GAME!
I FEEL BETTER! I'VE STOPPED SHAKING!
THE GAME'S OVER, CHARLIE BROWN, AND GUESS WHAT... WE WON!
LINUS TOOK YOUR PLACE... HE PITCHED A GREAT GAME... AND THERE WAS THIS LITTLE RED-HAIRED GIRL WATCHING...
SHE GOT SO EXCITED AFTER THE GAME THAT SHE RUSHED OUT TO THE MOUND, AND GAVE LINUS A BIG HUG!
AAUGH!
SCHULZ

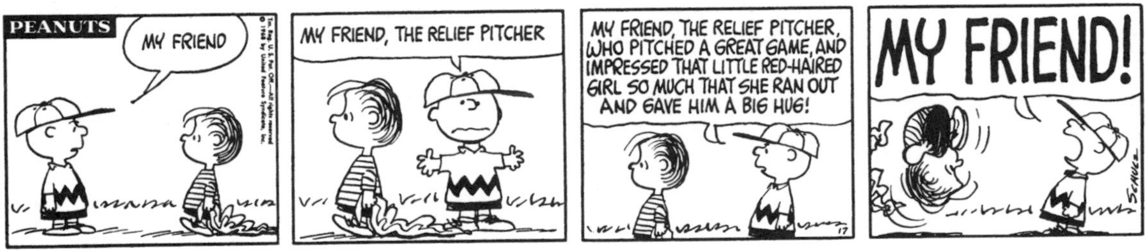
PEANUTS
MY FRIEND
MY FRIEND, THE RELIEF PITCHER
MY FRIEND, THE RELIEF PITCHER, WHO PITCHED A GREAT GAME, AND IMPRESSED THAT LITTLE RED-HAIRED GIRL SO MUCH THAT SHE RAN OUT AND GAVE HIM A BIG HUG!
MY FRIEND!
SCHULZ

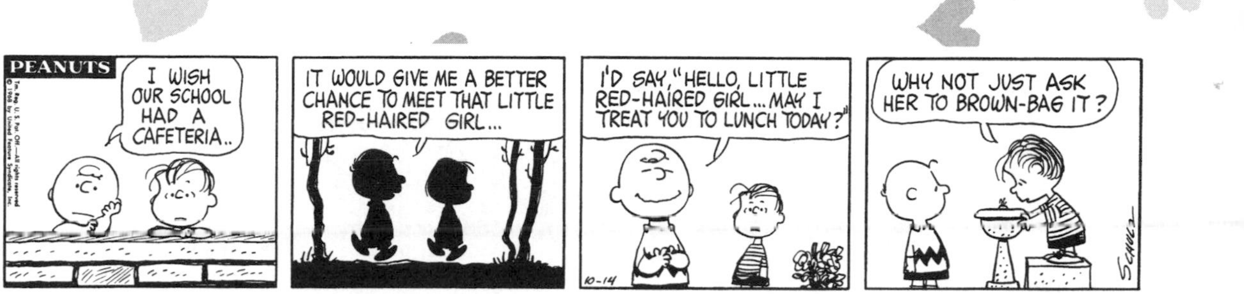
PEANUTS
I WISH OUR SCHOOL HAD A CAFETERIA..
IT WOULD GIVE ME A BETTER CHANCE TO MEET THAT LITTLE RED-HAIRED GIRL...
I'D SAY, "HELLO, LITTLE RED-HAIRED GIRL... MAY I TREAT YOU TO LUNCH TODAY?"
WHY NOT JUST ASK HER TO BROWN-BAG IT?

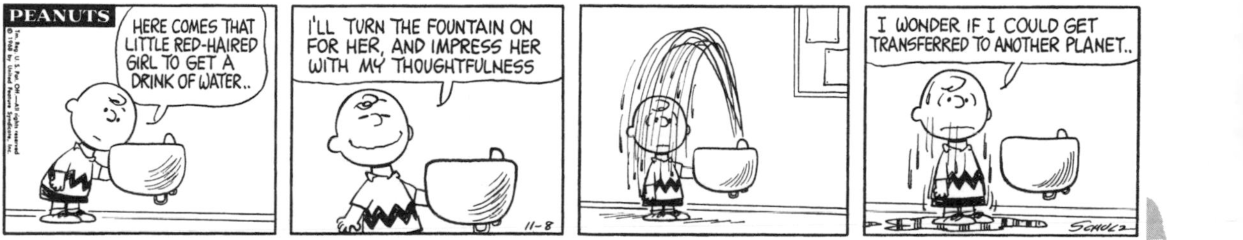
PEANUTS
HERE COMES THAT LITTLE RED-HAIRED GIRL TO GET A DRINK OF WATER..
I'LL TURN THE FOUNTAIN ON FOR HER, AND IMPRESS HER WITH MY THOUGHTFULNESS
I WONDER IF I COULD GET TRANSFERRED TO ANOTHER PLANET..

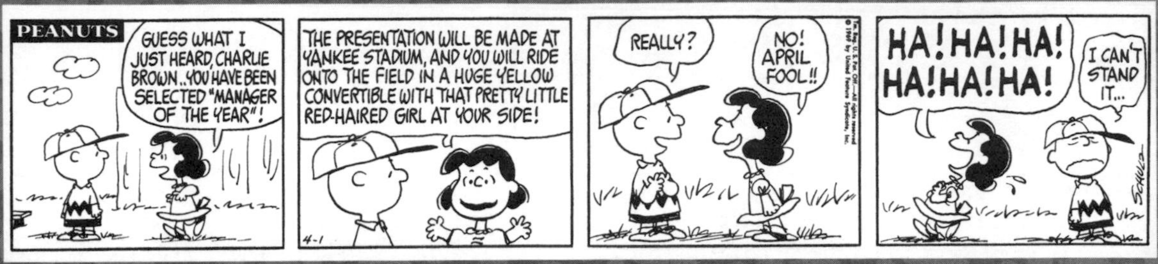
PEANUTS
GUESS WHAT I JUST HEARD, CHARLIE BROWN..YOU HAVE BEEN SELECTED "MANAGER OF THE YEAR"!
THE PRESENTATION WILL BE MADE AT YANKEE STADIUM, AND YOU WILL RIDE ONTO THE FIELD IN A HUGE YELLOW CONVERTIBLE WITH THAT PRETTY LITTLE RED-HAIRED GIRL AT YOUR SIDE!
4-1
REALLY?
NO! APRIL FOOL!!
HA! HA! HA! HA! HA! HA!
I CAN'T STAND IT...
SCHULZ

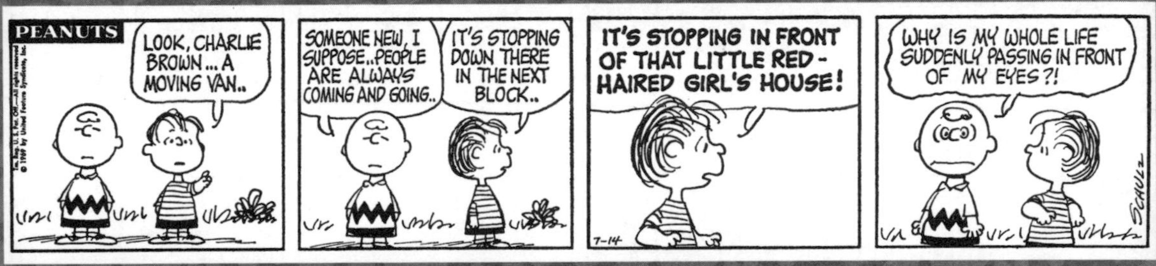
PEANUTS
LOOK, CHARLIE BROWN... A MOVING VAN..
SOMEONE NEW, I SUPPOSE..PEOPLE ARE ALWAYS COMING AND GOING..
IT'S STOPPING DOWN THERE IN THE NEXT BLOCK..
IT'S STOPPING IN FRONT OF THAT LITTLE RED-HAIRED GIRL'S HOUSE!
7-14
WHY IS MY WHOLE LIFE SUDDENLY PASSING IN FRONT OF MY EYES?!
SCHULZ

PEANUTS
Tm. Reg. U. S. Pat. Off.—All rights reserved
© 1969 by United Feature Syndicate, Inc.
THERE'S A MOVING VAN IN FRONT OF THAT LITTLE RED-HAIRED GIRL'S HOUSE!
SHE'S MOVING AWAY, CHARLIE BROWN... SEE? THEY'RE CARRYING OUT ALL THE FURNITURE!
IF SHE MOVES AWAY, YOU'LL NEVER SEE HER AGAIN.. YOU'VE GOT TO DO SOMETHING!
7-15
AAUGH!
I WAS HOPING FOR A MORE PRACTICAL RESPONSE
SCHULZ

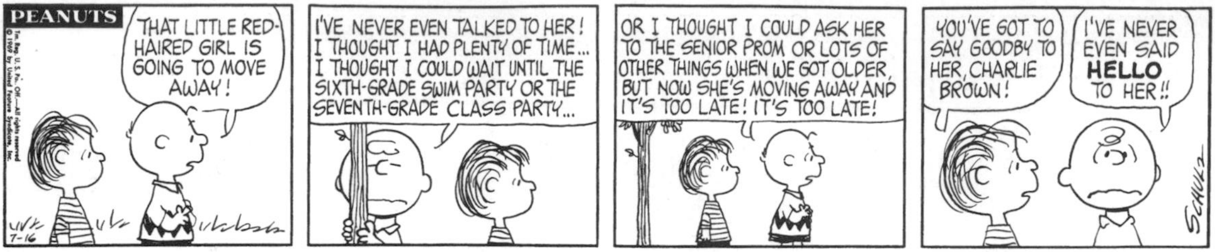
PEANUTS
THAT LITTLE RED-HAIRED GIRL IS GOING TO MOVE AWAY!
I'VE NEVER EVEN TALKED TO HER! I THOUGHT I HAD PLENTY OF TIME... I THOUGHT I COULD WAIT UNTIL THE SIXTH-GRADE SWIM PARTY OR THE SEVENTH-GRADE CLASS PARTY...
OR I THOUGHT I COULD ASK HER TO THE SENIOR PROM OR LOTS OF OTHER THINGS WHEN WE GOT OLDER, BUT NOW SHE'S MOVING AWAY AND IT'S TOO LATE! IT'S TOO LATE!
YOU'VE GOT TO SAY GOODBY TO HER, CHARLIE BROWN!
I'VE NEVER EVEN SAID **HELLO** TO HER!!

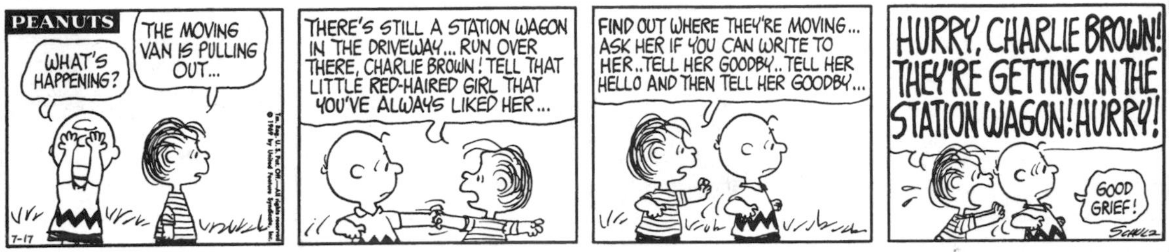
PEANUTS
WHAT'S HAPPENING?
THE MOVING VAN IS PULLING OUT...
THERE'S STILL A STATION WAGON IN THE DRIVEWAY... RUN OVER THERE, CHARLIE BROWN! TELL THAT LITTLE RED-HAIRED GIRL THAT YOU'VE ALWAYS LIKED HER...
FIND OUT WHERE THEY'RE MOVING... ASK HER IF YOU CAN WRITE TO HER.. TELL HER GOODBY.. TELL HER HELLO AND THEN TELL HER GOODBY...
HURRY, CHARLIE BROWN! THEY'RE GETTING IN THE STATION WAGON! HURRY!
GOOD GRIEF!

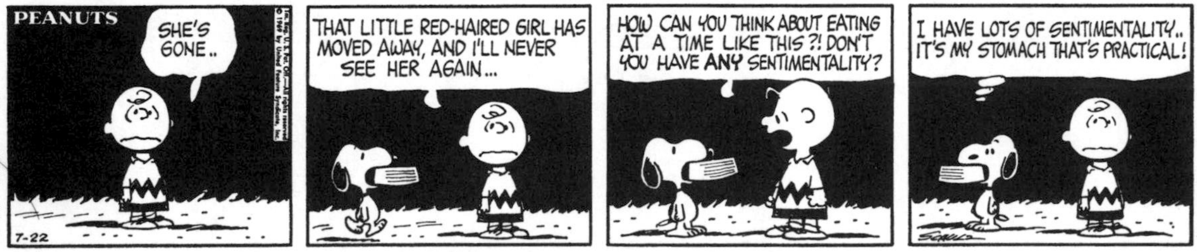
PEANUTS
SHE'S GONE..
THAT LITTLE RED-HAIRED GIRL HAS MOVED AWAY, AND I'LL NEVER SEE HER AGAIN...
HOW CAN YOU THINK ABOUT EATING AT A TIME LIKE THIS?! DON'T YOU HAVE **ANY** SENTIMENTALITY?
I HAVE LOTS OF SENTIMENTALITY.. IT'S MY STOMACH THAT'S PRACTICAL!

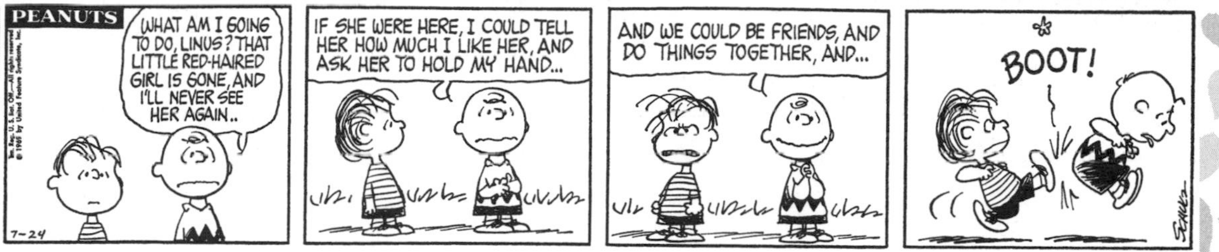
PEANUTS
WHAT AM I GOING TO DO, LINUS? THAT LITTLE RED-HAIRED GIRL IS GONE, AND I'LL NEVER SEE HER AGAIN..
7-24
IF SHE WERE HERE, I COULD TELL HER HOW MUCH I LIKE HER, AND ASK HER TO HOLD MY HAND...
AND WE COULD BE FRIENDS, AND DO THINGS TOGETHER, AND...
BOOT!
SCHULZ

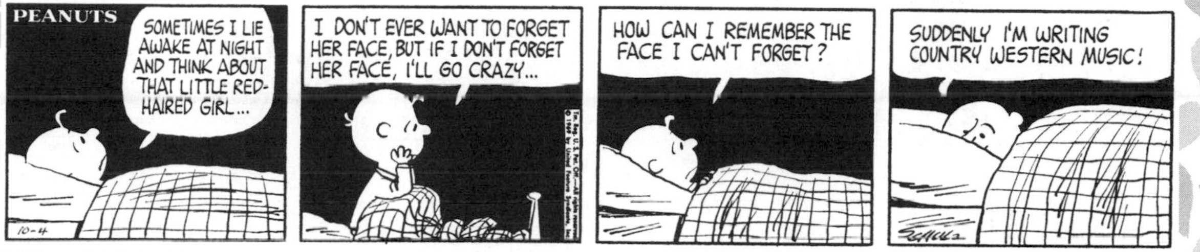
PEANUTS
SOMETIMES I LIE AWAKE AT NIGHT AND THINK ABOUT THAT LITTLE RED-HAIRED GIRL...
10-4
I DON'T EVER WANT TO FORGET HER FACE, BUT IF I DON'T FORGET HER FACE, I'LL GO CRAZY...
HOW CAN I REMEMBER THE FACE I CAN'T FORGET?
SUDDENLY I'M WRITING COUNTRY WESTERN MUSIC!
SCHULZ

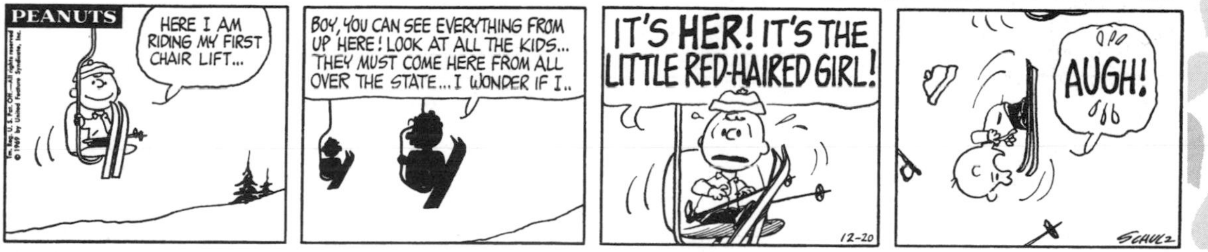
PEANUTS
HERE I AM RIDING MY FIRST CHAIR LIFT...
BOY, YOU CAN SEE EVERYTHING FROM UP HERE! LOOK AT ALL THE KIDS... THEY MUST COME HERE FROM ALL OVER THE STATE... I WONDER IF I..
IT'S HER! IT'S THE LITTLE RED-HAIRED GIRL!
12-20
AUGH!
SCHULZ

PEANUTS
WHAT HAPPENED? WHERE AM I?
YOU FELL OFF THE CHAIR LIFT, CHARLIE BROWN...ARE YOU ALL RIGHT?
I SAW HER! I SAW THE LITTLE RED-HAIRED GIRL! SHE WAS GOING DOWN THE LIFT WHILE I WAS GOING UP!!
I KNOW... I TALKED WITH HER... SHE JUST LEFT ON THE BUS TO GO BACK HOME....
Tm. Reg. U. S. Pat. Off.—All rights reserved
© 1969 by United Feature Syndicate, Inc.
12-22
AAUGHHH!!!
SCHULZ

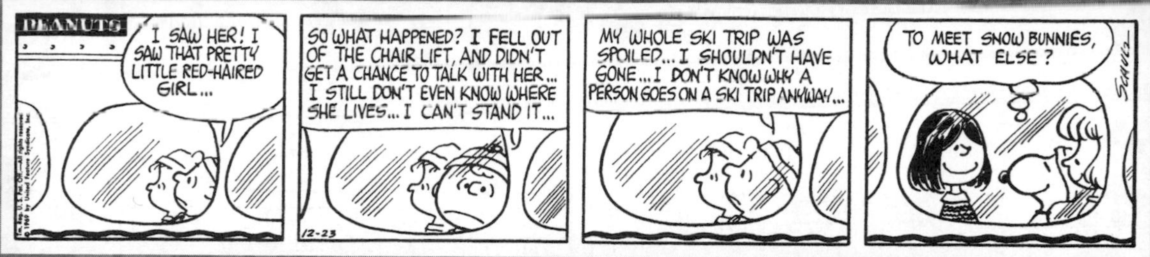
PEANUTS
I SAW HER! I SAW THAT PRETTY LITTLE RED-HAIRED GIRL...
SO WHAT HAPPENED? I FELL OUT OF THE CHAIR LIFT, AND DIDN'T GET A CHANCE TO TALK WITH HER... I STILL DON'T EVEN KNOW WHERE SHE LIVES... I CAN'T STAND IT...
12-23
MY WHOLE SKI TRIP WAS SPOILED... I SHOULDN'T HAVE GONE... I DON'T KNOW WHY A PERSON GOES ON A SKI TRIP ANYWAY...
TO MEET SNOW BUNNIES, WHAT ELSE ?

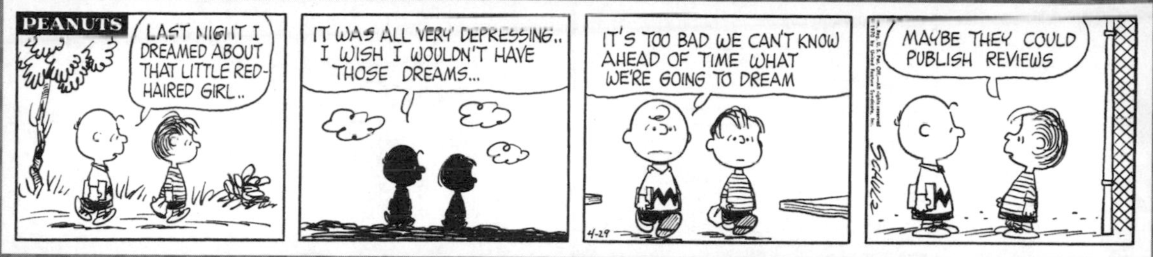
PEANUTS
LAST NIGHT I DREAMED ABOUT THAT LITTLE RED-HAIRED GIRL..
IT WAS ALL VERY DEPRESSING.. I WISH I WOULDN'T HAVE THOSE DREAMS...
IT'S TOO BAD WE CAN'T KNOW AHEAD OF TIME WHAT WE'RE GOING TO DREAM
4-29
MAYBE THEY COULD PUBLISH REVIEWS

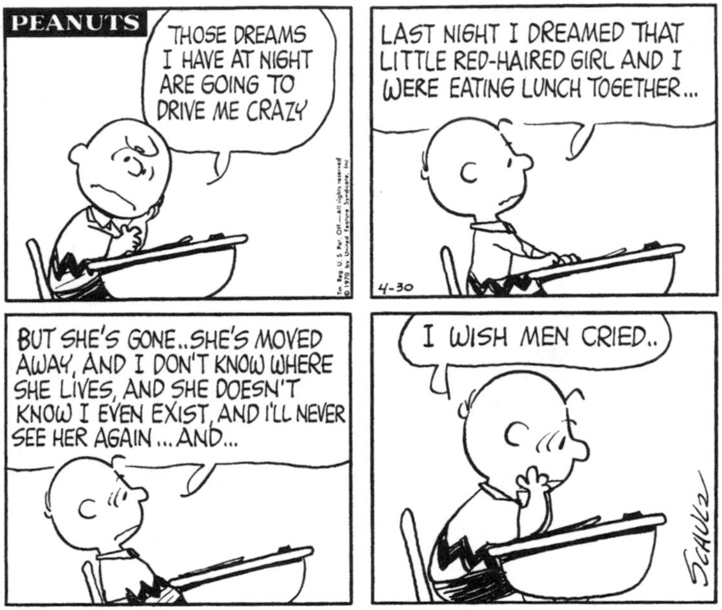
PEANUTS
THOSE DREAMS I HAVE AT NIGHT ARE GOING TO DRIVE ME CRAZY
Tm. Reg. U. S. Pat. Off.—All rights reserved
© 1970 by United Feature Syndicate, Inc
LAST NIGHT I DREAMED THAT LITTLE RED-HAIRED GIRL AND I WERE EATING LUNCH TOGETHER...
4-30
BUT SHE'S GONE..SHE'S MOVED AWAY, AND I DON'T KNOW WHERE SHE LIVES, AND SHE DOESN'T KNOW I EVEN EXIST, AND I'LL NEVER SEE HER AGAIN ... AND...
I WISH MEN CRIED..
SCHULZ

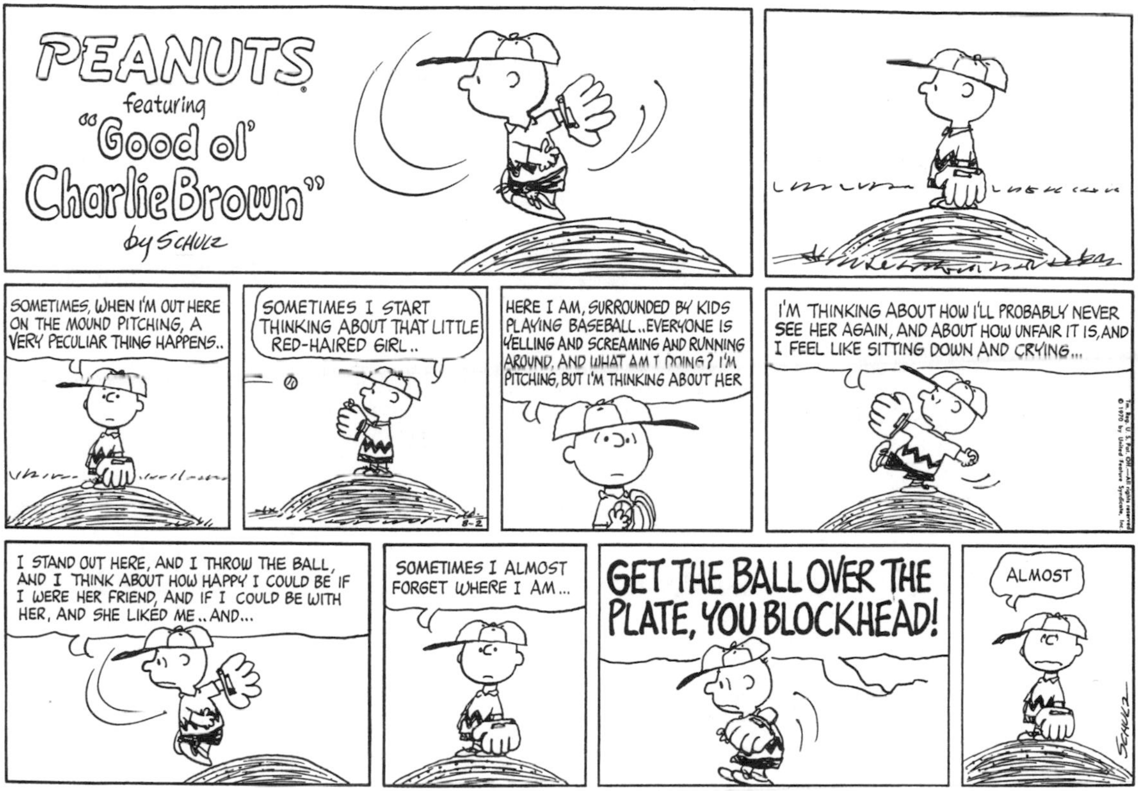
PEANUTS
featuring "Good ol' Charlie Brown"
by SCHULZ
SOMETIMES, WHEN I'M OUT HERE ON THE MOUND PITCHING, A VERY PECULIAR THING HAPPENS..
SOMETIMES I START THINKING ABOUT THAT LITTLE RED-HAIRED GIRL..
HERE I AM, SURROUNDED BY KIDS PLAYING BASEBALL..EVERYONE IS YELLING AND SCREAMING AND RUNNING AROUND, AND WHAT AM I DOING? I'M PITCHING, BUT I'M THINKING ABOUT HER
I'M THINKING ABOUT HOW I'LL PROBABLY NEVER SEE HER AGAIN, AND ABOUT HOW UNFAIR IT IS, AND I FEEL LIKE SITTING DOWN AND CRYING...
Tm. Reg. U. S. Pat. Off.—All rights reserved © 1970 by United Feature Syndicate, Inc.
I STAND OUT HERE, AND I THROW THE BALL, AND I THINK ABOUT HOW HAPPY I COULD BE IF I WERE HER FRIEND, AND IF I COULD BE WITH HER, AND SHE LIKED ME..AND...
SOMETIMES I ALMOST FORGET WHERE I AM...
GET THE BALL OVER THE PLATE, YOU BLOCKHEAD!
ALMOST
SCHULZ

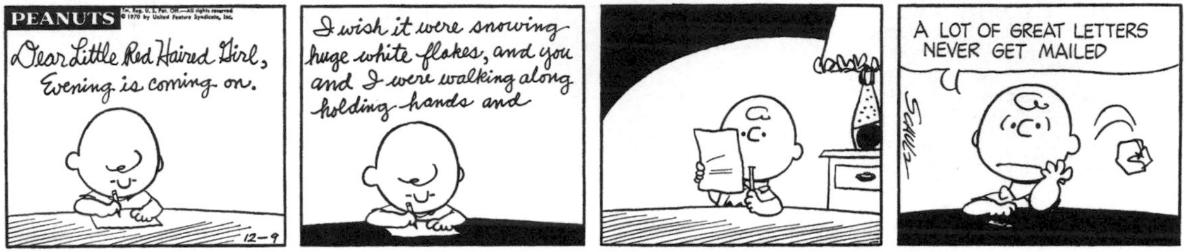
PEANUTS
Tm. Reg. U.S. Pat. Off.—All rights reserved © 1970 by United Feature Syndicate, Inc.
Dear Little Red Haired Girl,
Evening is coming on.
12-9
I wish it were snowing huge white flakes, and you and I were walking along holding hands and
A LOT OF GREAT LETTERS NEVER GET MAILED
SCHULZ

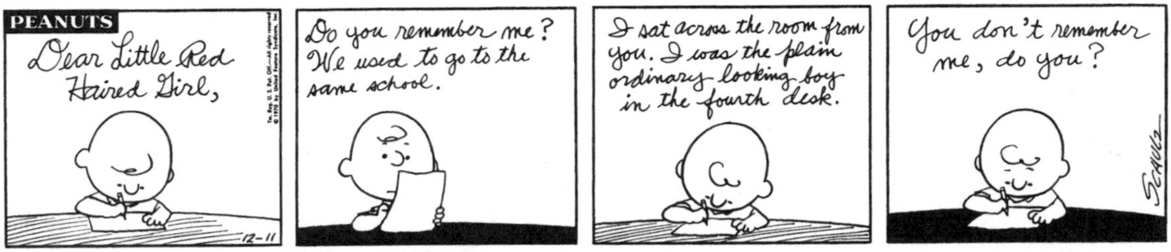
PEANUTS
Dear Little Red Haired Girl,
12-11
Do you remember me? We used to go to the same school.
I sat across the room from you. I was the plain ordinary looking boy in the fourth desk.
You don't remember me, do you?
SCHULZ

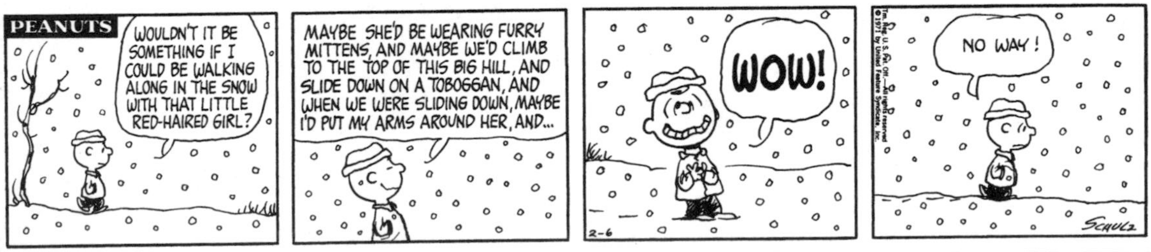
PEANUTS
WOULDN'T IT BE SOMETHING IF I COULD BE WALKING ALONG IN THE SNOW WITH THAT LITTLE RED-HAIRED GIRL?
MAYBE SHE'D BE WEARING FURRY MITTENS, AND MAYBE WE'D CLIMB TO THE TOP OF THIS BIG HILL, AND SLIDE DOWN ON A TOBOGGAN, AND WHEN WE WERE SLIDING DOWN, MAYBE I'D PUT MY ARMS AROUND HER, AND...
WOW!
2-6
NO WAY!
SCHULZ

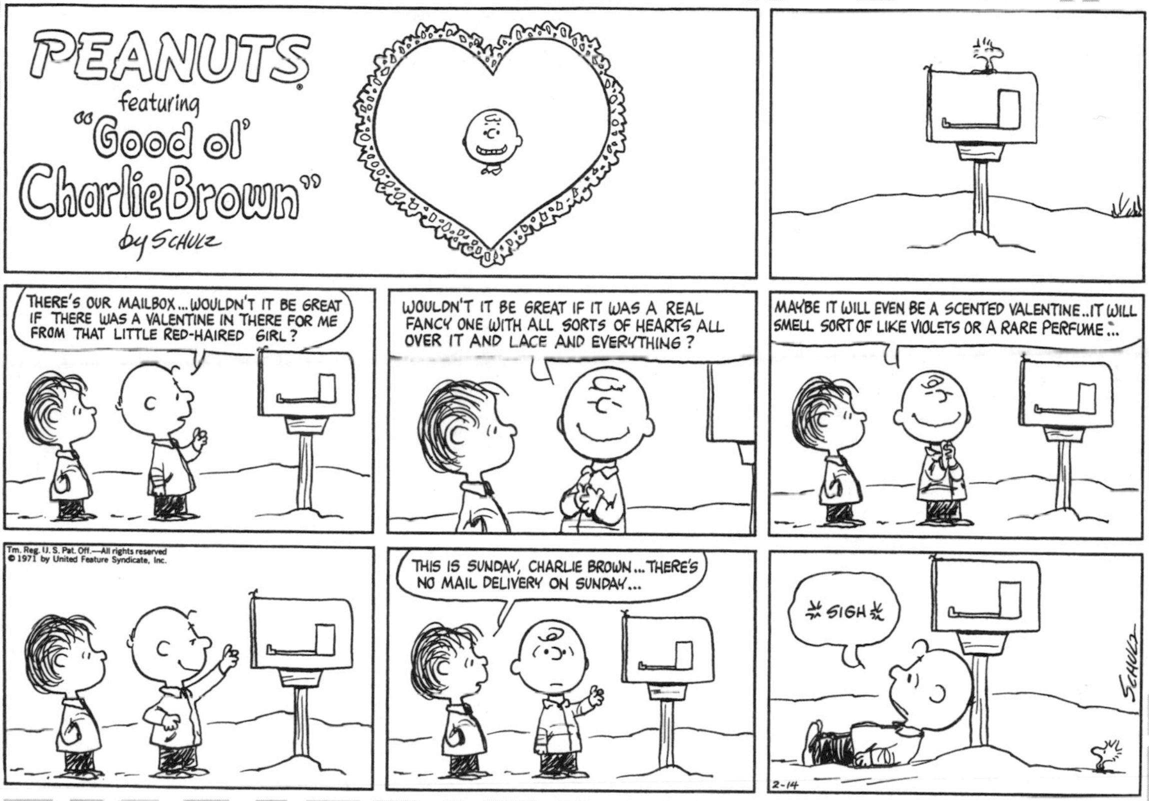
PEANUTS
featuring "Good ol' Charlie Brown"
by SCHULZ
THERE'S OUR MAILBOX... WOULDN'T IT BE GREAT IF THERE WAS A VALENTINE IN THERE FOR ME FROM THAT LITTLE RED-HAIRED GIRL?
WOULDN'T IT BE GREAT IF IT WAS A REAL FANCY ONE WITH ALL SORTS OF HEARTS ALL OVER IT AND LACE AND EVERYTHING?
MAYBE IT WILL EVEN BE A SCENTED VALENTINE.. IT WILL SMELL SORT OF LIKE VIOLETS OR A RARE PERFUME...
Tm. Reg. U. S. Pat. Off.—All rights reserved
© 1971 by United Feature Syndicate, Inc.
THIS IS SUNDAY, CHARLIE BROWN... THERE'S NO MAIL DELIVERY ON SUNDAY...
SIGH
SCHULZ
2-14

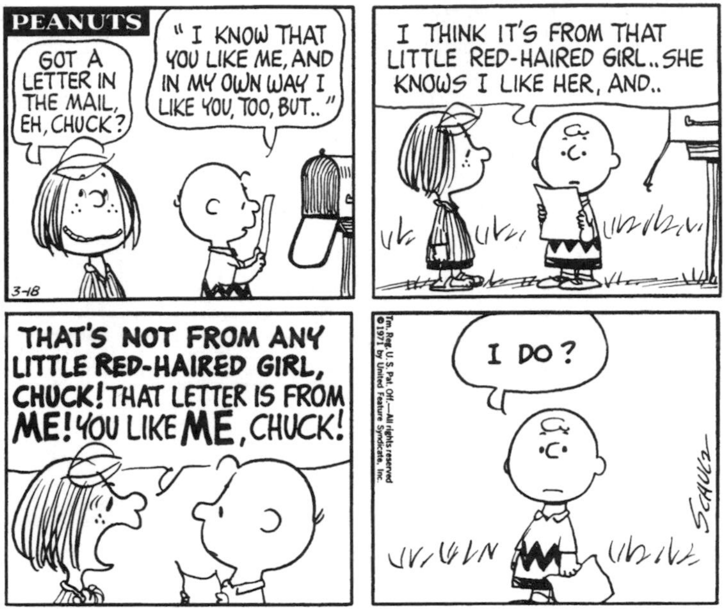
PEANUTS
GOT A LETTER IN THE MAIL, EH, CHUCK?
" I KNOW THAT YOU LIKE ME, AND IN MY OWN WAY I LIKE YOU, TOO, BUT.."
3-18
I THINK IT'S FROM THAT LITTLE RED-HAIRED GIRL.. SHE KNOWS I LIKE HER, AND..
THAT'S NOT FROM ANY LITTLE RED-HAIRED GIRL, CHUCK! THAT LETTER IS FROM ME! YOU LIKE ME, CHUCK!
Tm. Reg. U. S. Pat. Off.—All rights reserved
© 1971 by United Feature Syndicate, Inc.
I DO?
SCHULZ

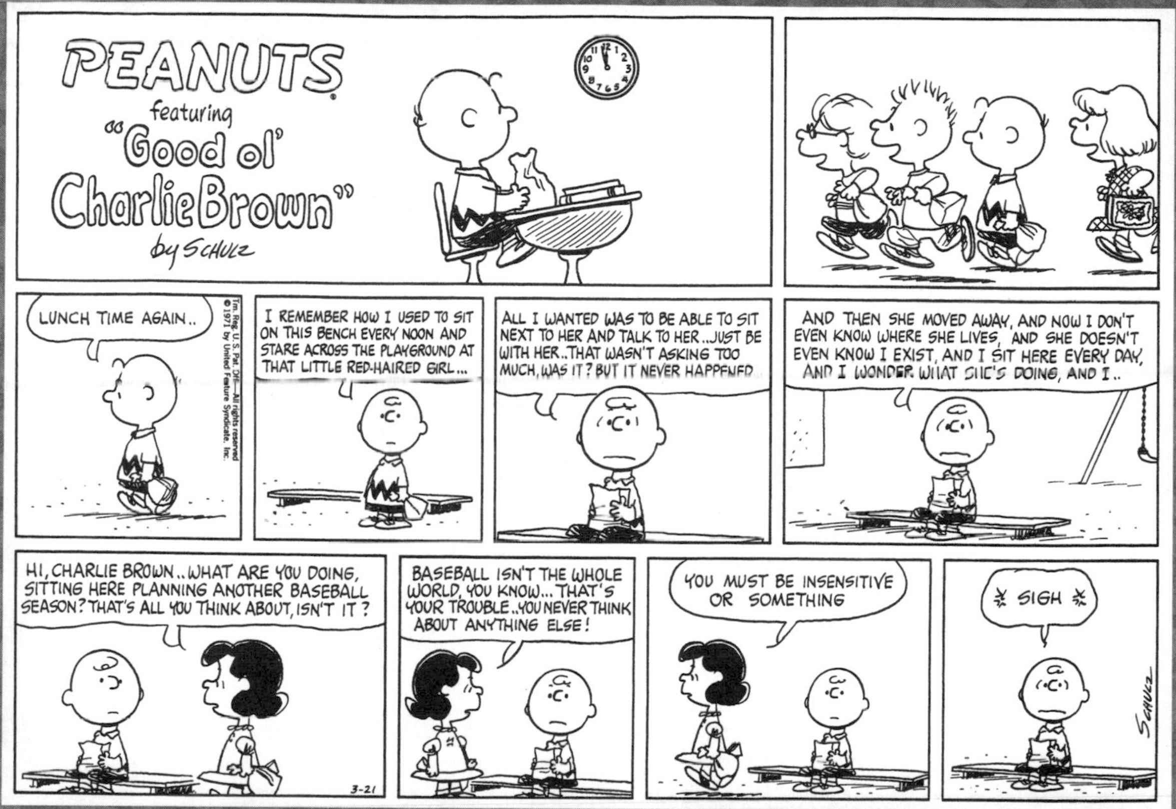
PEANUTS featuring "Good ol' Charlie Brown" by SCHULZ
Tm. Reg. U.S. Pat. Off.—All rights reserved © 1971 by United Feature Syndicate, Inc.
LUNCH TIME AGAIN..
I REMEMBER HOW I USED TO SIT ON THIS BENCH EVERY NOON AND STARE ACROSS THE PLAYGROUND AT THAT LITTLE RED-HAIRED GIRL...
ALL I WANTED WAS TO BE ABLE TO SIT NEXT TO HER AND TALK TO HER..JUST BE WITH HER..THAT WASN'T ASKING TOO MUCH, WAS IT? BUT IT NEVER HAPPENED
AND THEN SHE MOVED AWAY, AND NOW I DON'T EVEN KNOW WHERE SHE LIVES, AND SHE DOESN'T EVEN KNOW I EXIST, AND I SIT HERE EVERY DAY, AND I WONDER WHAT SHE'S DOING, AND I..
HI, CHARLIE BROWN..WHAT ARE YOU DOING, SITTING HERE PLANNING ANOTHER BASEBALL SEASON? THAT'S ALL YOU THINK ABOUT, ISN'T IT?
3-21
BASEBALL ISN'T THE WHOLE WORLD, YOU KNOW... THAT'S YOUR TROUBLE..YOU NEVER THINK ABOUT ANYTHING ELSE!
YOU MUST BE INSENSITIVE OR SOMETHING
SIGH
SCHULZ

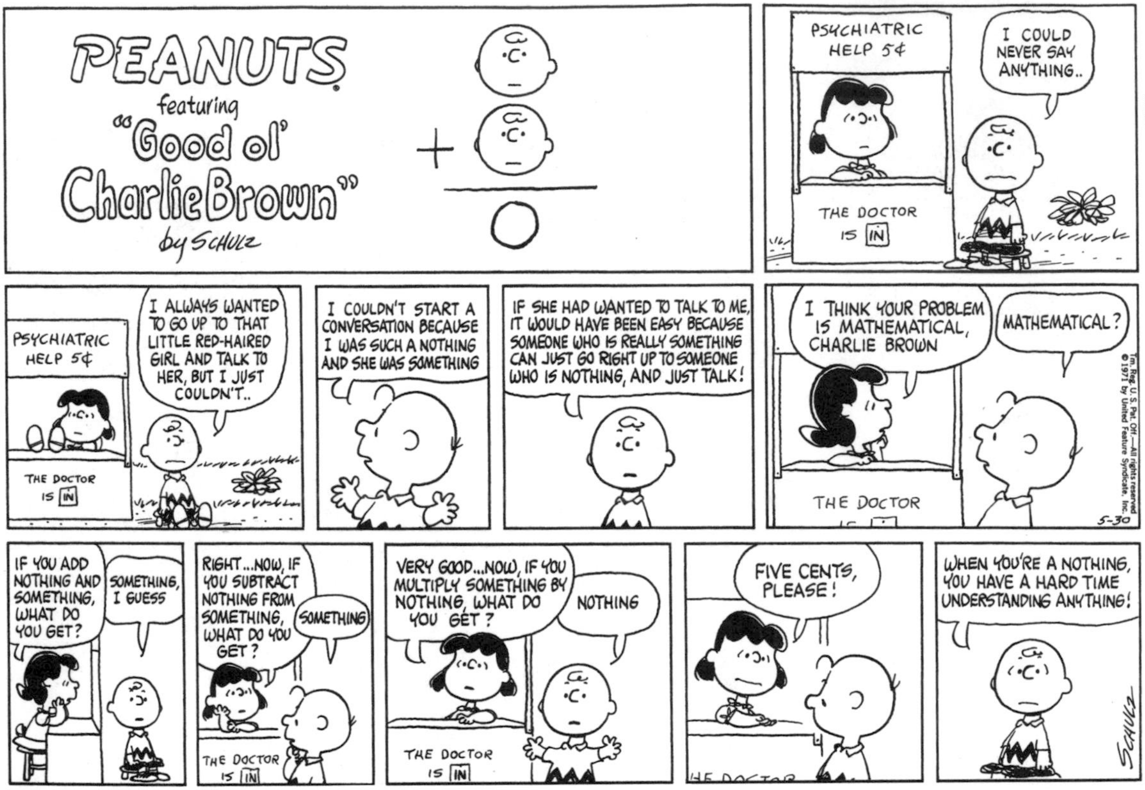
PEANUTS
featuring "Good ol' Charlie Brown"
by SCHULZ
PSYCHIATRIC HELP 5¢
I COULD NEVER SAY ANYTHING..
THE DOCTOR IS IN
PSYCHIATRIC HELP 5¢
I ALWAYS WANTED TO GO UP TO THAT LITTLE RED-HAIRED GIRL AND TALK TO HER, BUT I JUST COULDN'T..
THE DOCTOR IS IN
I COULDN'T START A CONVERSATION BECAUSE I WAS SUCH A NOTHING AND SHE WAS SOMETHING
IF SHE HAD WANTED TO TALK TO ME, IT WOULD HAVE BEEN EASY BECAUSE SOMEONE WHO IS REALLY SOMETHING CAN JUST GO RIGHT UP TO SOMEONE WHO IS NOTHING, AND JUST TALK!
I THINK YOUR PROBLEM IS MATHEMATICAL, CHARLIE BROWN
MATHEMATICAL?
THE DOCTOR
Tm. Reg. U.S. Pat. Off.—All rights reserved © 1971 by United Feature Syndicate, Inc.
5-30
IF YOU ADD NOTHING AND SOMETHING, WHAT DO YOU GET?
SOMETHING, I GUESS
RIGHT...NOW, IF YOU SUBTRACT NOTHING FROM SOMETHING, WHAT DO YOU GET?
SOMETHING
THE DOCTOR IS IN
VERY GOOD...NOW, IF YOU MULTIPLY SOMETHING BY NOTHING, WHAT DO YOU GET?
NOTHING
THE DOCTOR IS IN
FIVE CENTS, PLEASE!
WHEN YOU'RE A NOTHING, YOU HAVE A HARD TIME UNDERSTANDING ANYTHING!
SCHULZ

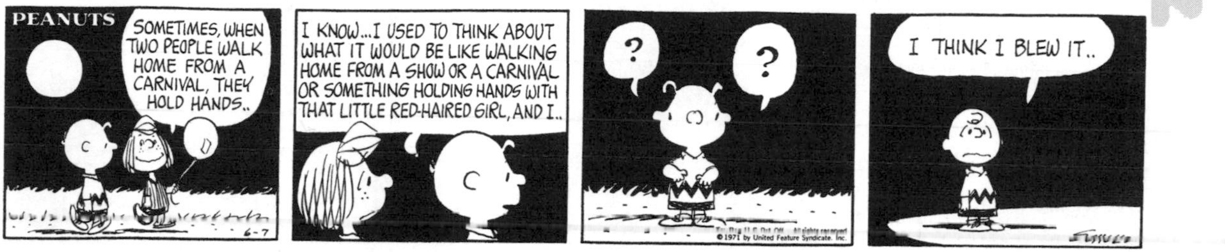
PEANUTS
SOMETIMES, WHEN TWO PEOPLE WALK HOME FROM A CARNIVAL, THEY HOLD HANDS..
I KNOW...I USED TO THINK ABOUT WHAT IT WOULD BE LIKE WALKING HOME FROM A SHOW OR A CARNIVAL OR SOMETHING HOLDING HANDS WITH THAT LITTLE RED-HAIRED GIRL, AND I..
?
?
© 1971 by United Feature Syndicate, Inc.
I THINK I BLEW IT..

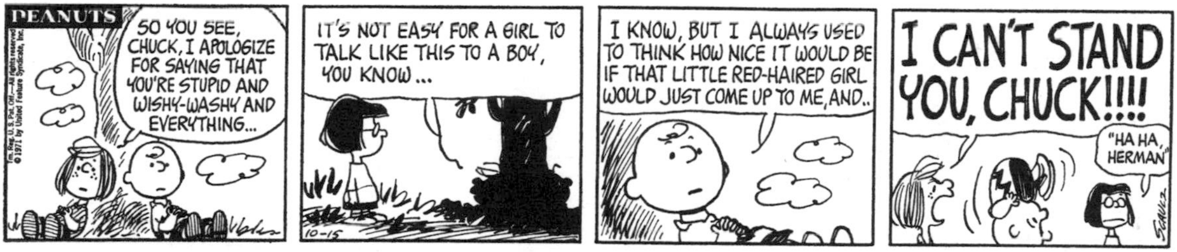
PEANUTS
SO YOU SEE, CHUCK, I APOLOGIZE FOR SAYING THAT YOU'RE STUPID AND WISHY-WASHY AND EVERYTHING...
IT'S NOT EASY FOR A GIRL TO TALK LIKE THIS TO A BOY, YOU KNOW...
I KNOW, BUT I ALWAYS USED TO THINK HOW NICE IT WOULD BE IF THAT LITTLE RED-HAIRED GIRL WOULD JUST COME UP TO ME, AND..
I CAN'T STAND YOU, CHUCK!!!!
"HA HA, HERMAN"

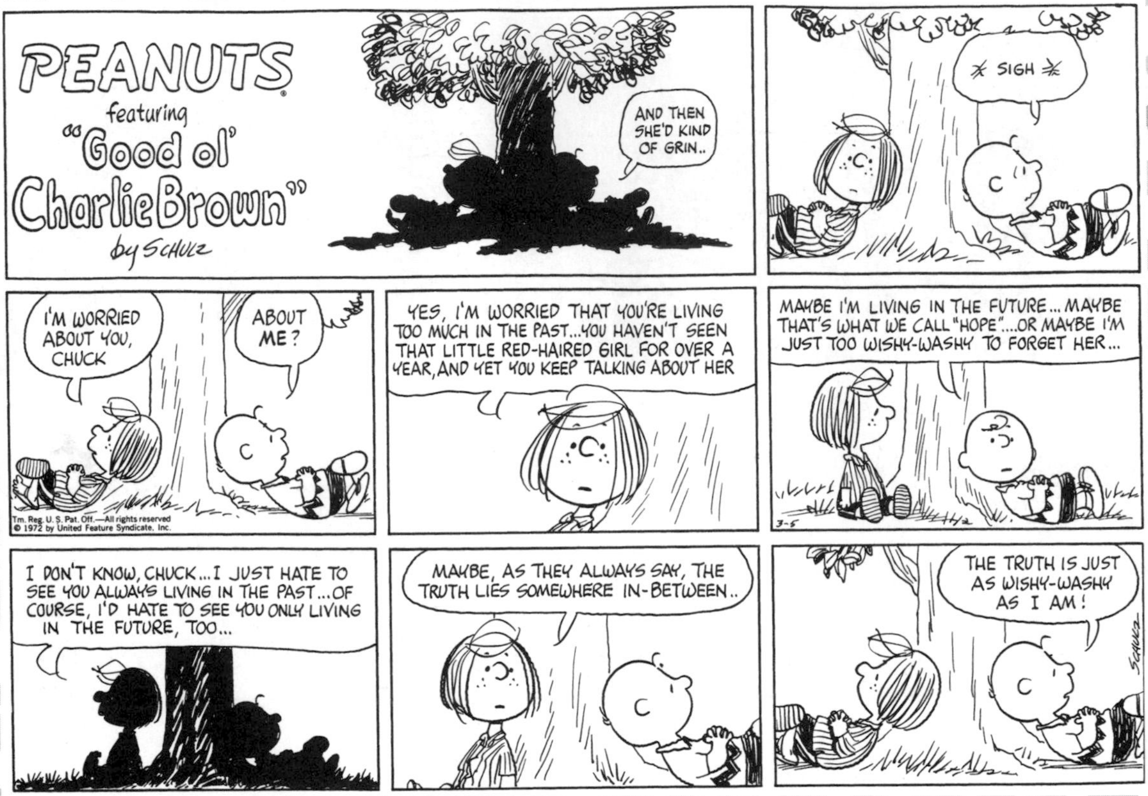
PEANUTS
featuring
"Good ol' Charlie Brown"
by SCHULZ
AND THEN SHE'D KIND OF GRIN..
* SIGH *
I'M WORRIED ABOUT YOU, CHUCK
ABOUT ME?
YES, I'M WORRIED THAT YOU'RE LIVING TOO MUCH IN THE PAST...YOU HAVEN'T SEEN THAT LITTLE RED-HAIRED GIRL FOR OVER A YEAR, AND YET YOU KEEP TALKING ABOUT HER
MAYBE I'M LIVING IN THE FUTURE... MAYBE THAT'S WHAT WE CALL "HOPE"....OR MAYBE I'M JUST TOO WISHY-WASHY TO FORGET HER...
I DON'T KNOW, CHUCK... I JUST HATE TO SEE YOU ALWAYS LIVING IN THE PAST...OF COURSE, I'D HATE TO SEE YOU ONLY LIVING IN THE FUTURE, TOO...
MAYBE, AS THEY ALWAYS SAY, THE TRUTH LIES SOMEWHERE IN-BETWEEN..
THE TRUTH IS JUST AS WISHY-WASHY AS I AM!
Tm. Reg. U. S. Pat. Off.—All rights reserved © 1972 by United Feature Syndicate, Inc.
3-5
SCHULZ

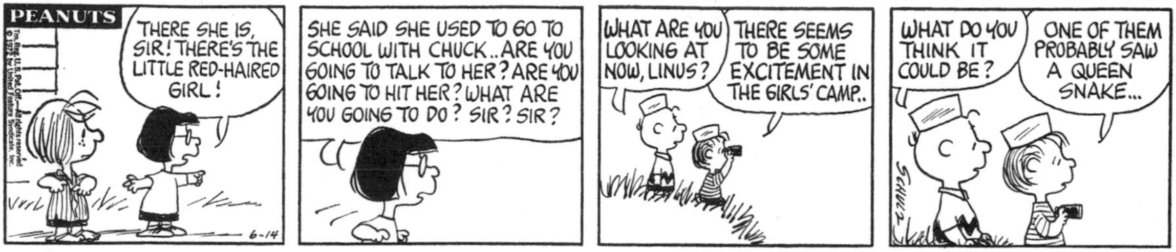
PEANUTS
Tm. Reg. U.S. Pat. Off.—All rights reserved © 1972 by United Feature Syndicate, Inc.
THERE SHE IS, SIR! THERE'S THE LITTLE RED-HAIRED GIRL!
6-14
SHE SAID SHE USED TO GO TO SCHOOL WITH CHUCK..ARE YOU GOING TO TALK TO HER? ARE YOU GOING TO HIT HER? WHAT ARE YOU GOING TO DO? SIR? SIR?
WHAT ARE YOU LOOKING AT NOW, LINUS?
THERE SEEMS TO BE SOME EXCITEMENT IN THE GIRLS' CAMP..
WHAT DO YOU THINK IT COULD BE?
ONE OF THEM PROBABLY SAW A QUEEN SNAKE...
SCHULZ

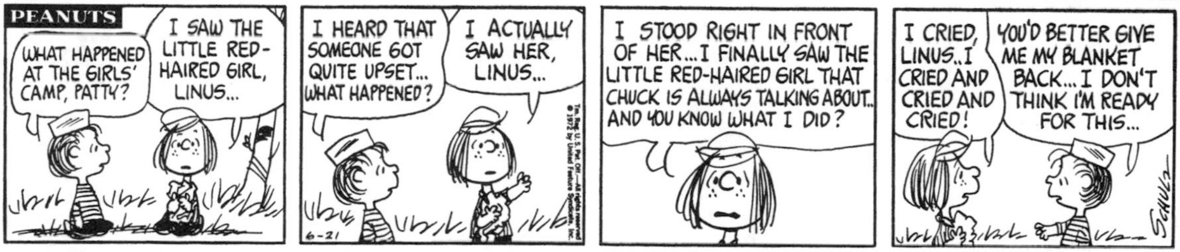
PEANUTS
WHAT HAPPENED AT THE GIRLS' CAMP, PATTY?
I SAW THE LITTLE RED-HAIRED GIRL, LINUS...
I HEARD THAT SOMEONE GOT QUITE UPSET... WHAT HAPPENED?
I ACTUALLY SAW HER, LINUS...
6-21
Tm. Reg. U.S. Pat. Off.—All rights reserved © 1972 by United Feature Syndicate, Inc.
I STOOD RIGHT IN FRONT OF HER...I FINALLY SAW THE LITTLE RED-HAIRED GIRL THAT CHUCK IS ALWAYS TALKING ABOUT.. AND YOU KNOW WHAT I DID?
I CRIED, LINUS..I CRIED AND CRIED AND CRIED!
YOU'D BETTER GIVE ME MY BLANKET BACK...I DON'T THINK I'M READY FOR THIS...
SCHULZ

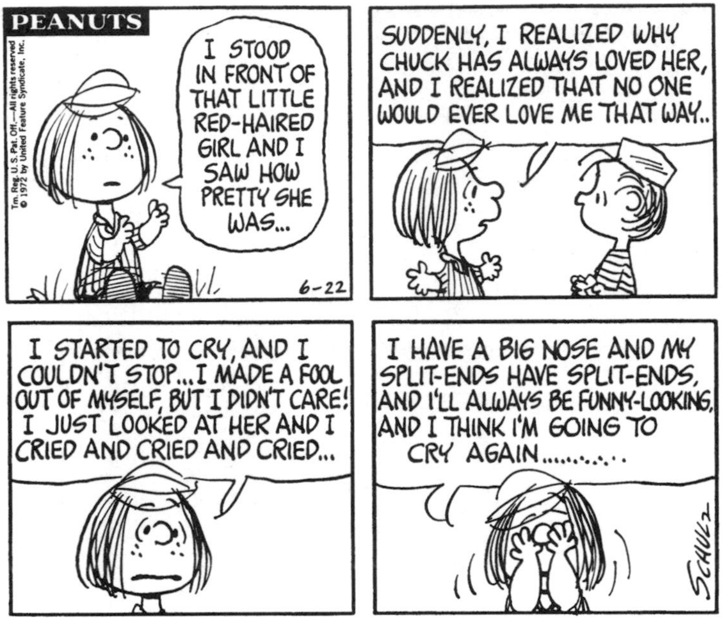
PEANUTS
Tm. Reg. U. S. Pat. Off.—All rights reserved © 1972 by United Feature Syndicate, Inc.
I STOOD IN FRONT OF THAT LITTLE RED-HAIRED GIRL AND I SAW HOW PRETTY SHE WAS...
6-22
SUDDENLY, I REALIZED WHY CHUCK HAS ALWAYS LOVED HER, AND I REALIZED THAT NO ONE WOULD EVER LOVE ME THAT WAY..
I STARTED TO CRY, AND I COULDN'T STOP...I MADE A FOOL OUT OF MYSELF, BUT I DIDN'T CARE! I JUST LOOKED AT HER AND I CRIED AND CRIED AND CRIED...
I HAVE A BIG NOSE AND MY SPLIT-ENDS HAVE SPLIT-ENDS, AND I'LL ALWAYS BE FUNNY-LOOKING, AND I THINK I'M GOING TO CRY AGAIN..........
SCHULZ

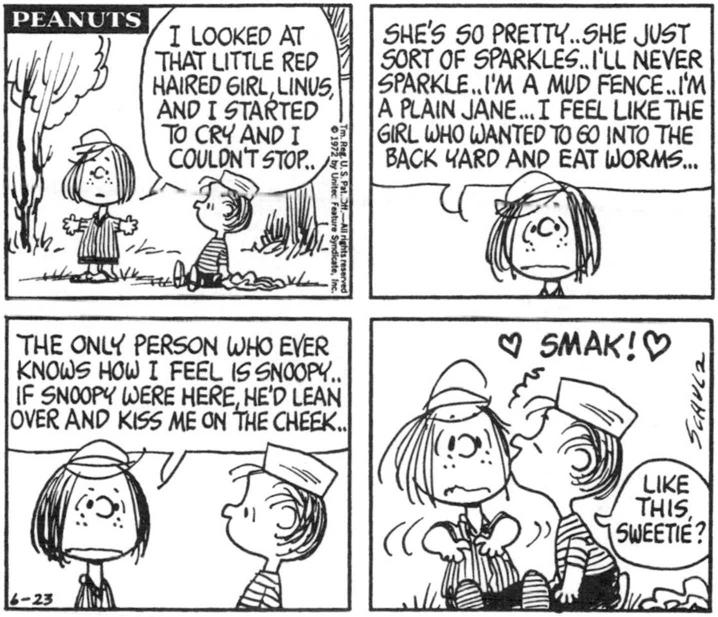
PEANUTS
I LOOKED AT THAT LITTLE RED HAIRED GIRL, LINUS, AND I STARTED TO CRY AND I COULDN'T STOP..
Tm. Reg. U. S. Pat. Off.—All rights reserved © 1972 by United Feature Syndicate, Inc.
SHE'S SO PRETTY..SHE JUST SORT OF SPARKLES..I'LL NEVER SPARKLE..I'M A MUD FENCE..I'M A PLAIN JANE...I FEEL LIKE THE GIRL WHO WANTED TO GO INTO THE BACK YARD AND EAT WORMS...
THE ONLY PERSON WHO EVER KNOWS HOW I FEEL IS SNOOPY.. IF SNOOPY WERE HERE, HE'D LEAN OVER AND KISS ME ON THE CHEEK..
6-23
SMAK!
SCHULZ
LIKE THIS, SWEETIE?

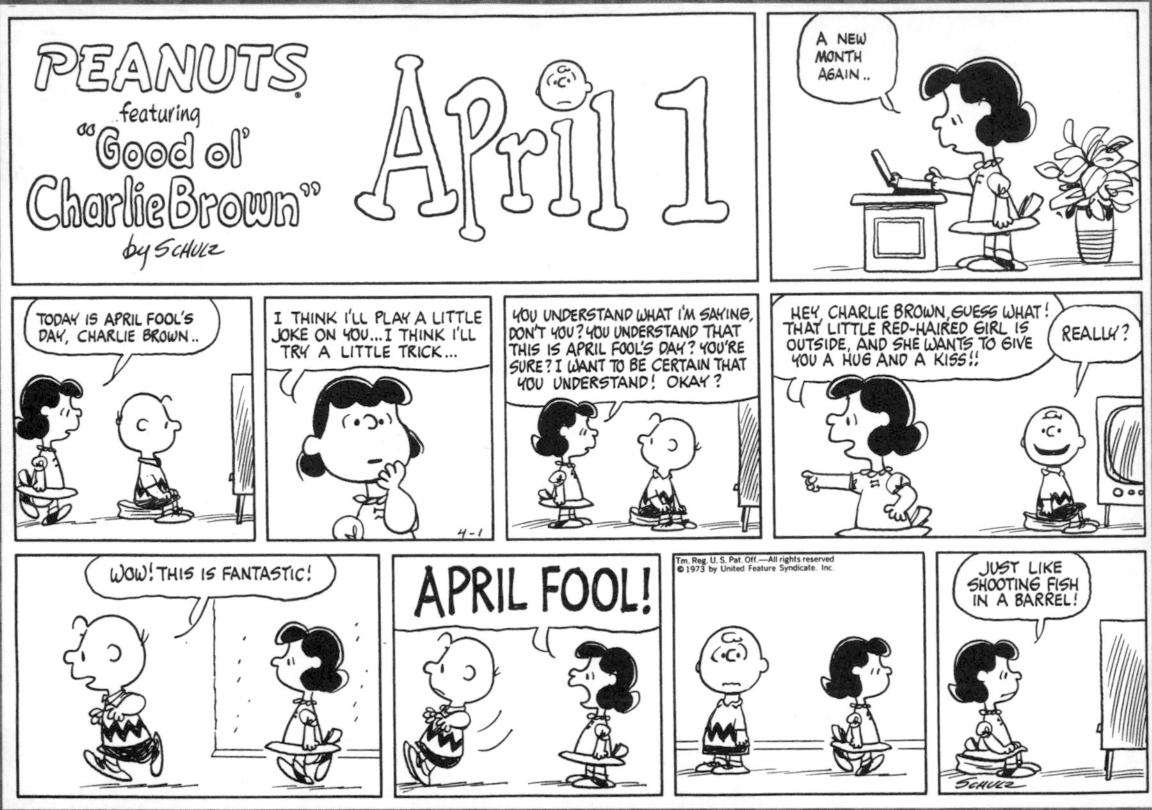
PEANUTS
featuring
"Good ol' Charlie Brown"
by SCHULZ
April 1
A NEW MONTH AGAIN..
TODAY IS APRIL FOOL'S DAY, CHARLIE BROWN..
I THINK I'LL PLAY A LITTLE JOKE ON YOU...I THINK I'LL TRY A LITTLE TRICK...
YOU UNDERSTAND WHAT I'M SAYING, DON'T YOU? YOU UNDERSTAND THAT THIS IS APRIL FOOL'S DAY? YOU'RE SURE? I WANT TO BE CERTAIN THAT YOU UNDERSTAND! OKAY?
HEY, CHARLIE BROWN, GUESS WHAT! THAT LITTLE RED-HAIRED GIRL IS OUTSIDE, AND SHE WANTS TO GIVE YOU A HUG AND A KISS!!
REALLY?
WOW! THIS IS FANTASTIC!
APRIL FOOL!
Tm. Reg. U.S. Pat. Off.—All rights reserved
© 1973 by United Feature Syndicate, Inc.
JUST LIKE SHOOTING FISH IN A BARREL!
SCHULZ

I'M ALWAYS THINKING ABOUT THAT LITTLE RED HAIRED GIRL, BUT I KNOW SHE DOESN'T THINK OF ME
SHE DOESN'T THINK OF ME BECAUSE I'M A NOTHING, AND YOU CAN'T THINK OF NOTHING!
5-30
YOU'RE NOT REALLY A NOTHING, CHARLIE BROWN
ALMOST
© 1978 United Feature Syndicate, Inc.
DOES A GIRL EVER GO AROUND THINKING OF A .00001 ?!
SCHULZ

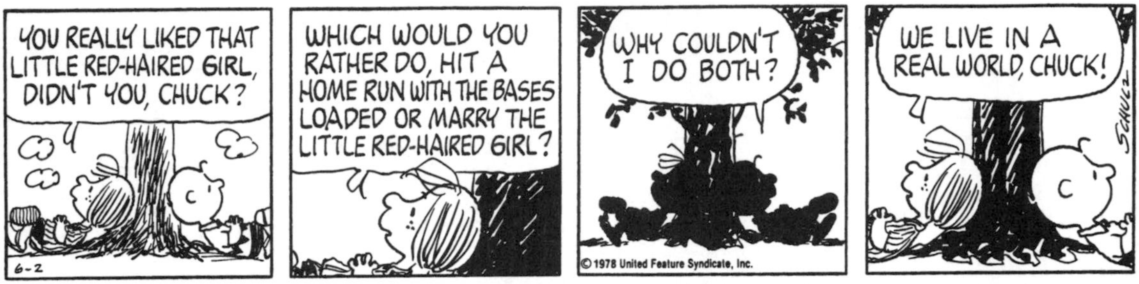
YOU REALLY LIKED THAT LITTLE RED-HAIRED GIRL, DIDN'T YOU, CHUCK?
WHICH WOULD YOU RATHER DO, HIT A HOME RUN WITH THE BASES LOADED OR MARRY THE LITTLE RED-HAIRED GIRL?
WHY COULDN'T I DO BOTH?
WE LIVE IN A REAL WORLD, CHUCK!
6-2
© 1978 United Feature Syndicate, Inc.
SCHULZ

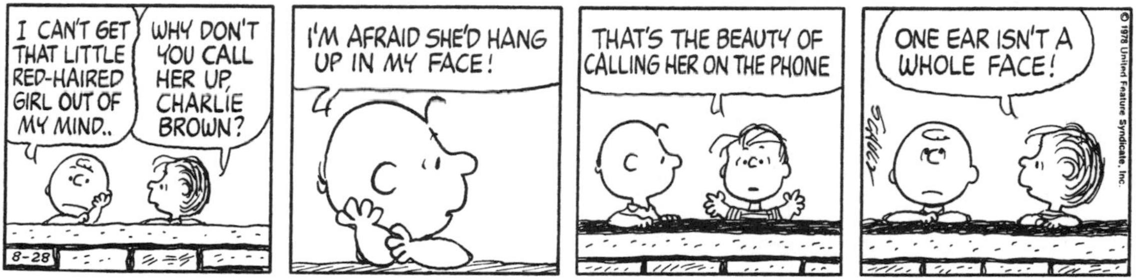

I CAN'T GET THAT LITTLE RED-HAIRED GIRL OUT OF MY MIND..
WHY DON'T YOU CALL HER UP, CHARLIE BROWN?
8-28
I'M AFRAID SHE'D HANG UP IN MY FACE!
THAT'S THE BEAUTY OF CALLING HER ON THE PHONE
ONE EAR ISN'T A WHOLE FACE!
SCHULZ
© 1978 United Feature Syndicate, Inc.

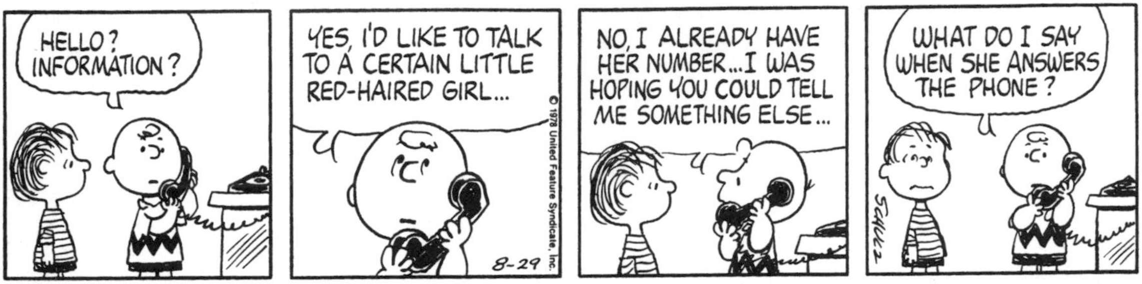
HELLO? INFORMATION?
YES, I'D LIKE TO TALK TO A CERTAIN LITTLE RED-HAIRED GIRL...
© 1978 United Feature Syndicate, Inc.
8-29
NO, I ALREADY HAVE HER NUMBER...I WAS HOPING YOU COULD TELL ME SOMETHING ELSE...
WHAT DO I SAY WHEN SHE ANSWERS THE PHONE?
SCHULZ

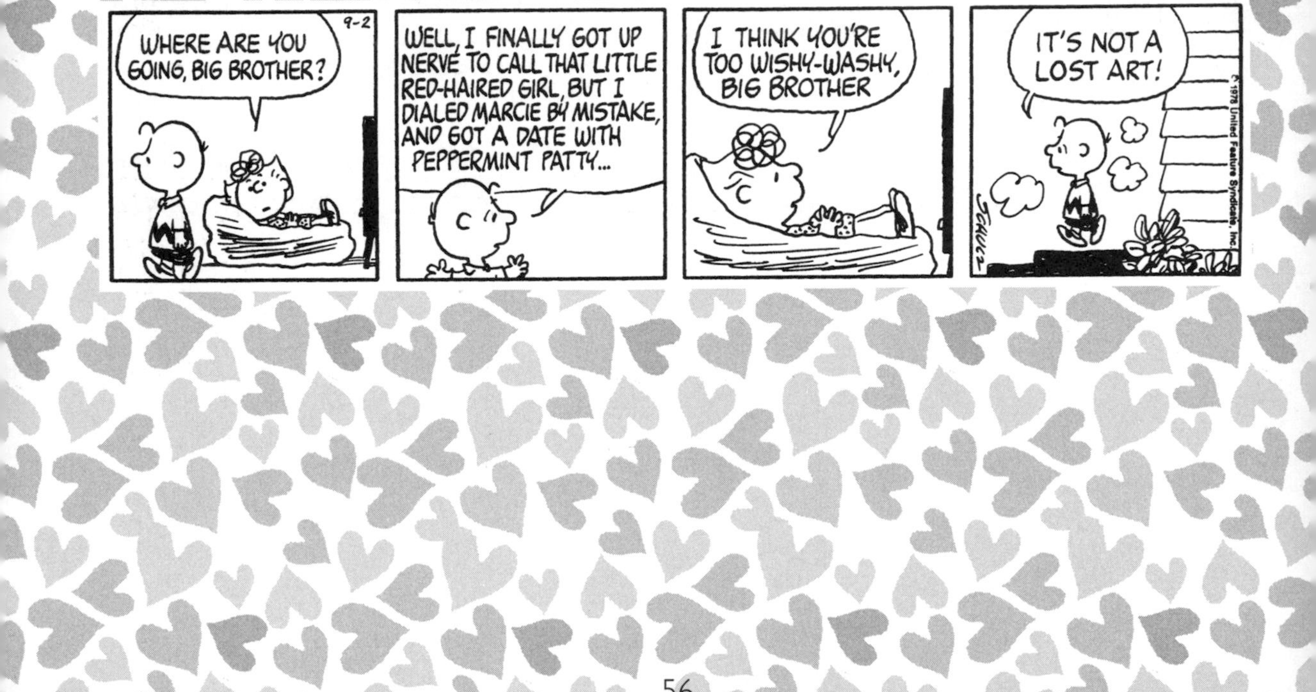
9-2
WHERE ARE YOU GOING, BIG BROTHER?
WELL, I FINALLY GOT UP NERVE TO CALL THAT LITTLE RED-HAIRED GIRL, BUT I DIALED MARCIE BY MISTAKE, AND GOT A DATE WITH PEPPERMINT PATTY...
I THINK YOU'RE TOO WISHY-WASHY, BIG BROTHER
SCHULZ
IT'S NOT A LOST ART!
© 1978 United Feature Syndicate, Inc.

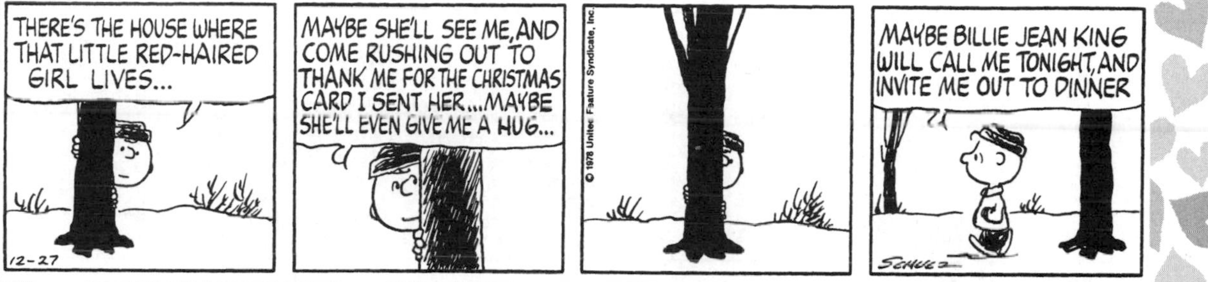
THERE'S THE HOUSE WHERE THAT LITTLE RED-HAIRED GIRL LIVES...
MAYBE SHE'LL SEE ME, AND COME RUSHING OUT TO THANK ME FOR THE CHRISTMAS CARD I SENT HER...MAYBE SHE'LL EVEN GIVE ME A HUG...
MAYBE BILLIE JEAN KING WILL CALL ME TONIGHT, AND INVITE ME OUT TO DINNER
12-27
SCHULZ
© 1978 United Feature Syndicate, Inc.

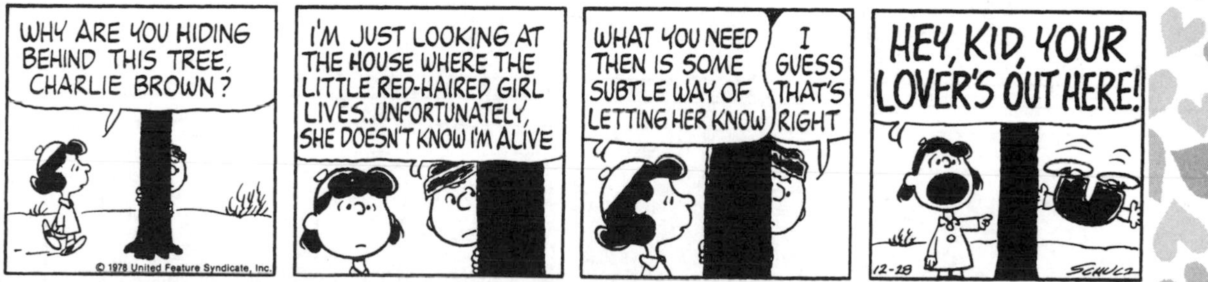
WHY ARE YOU HIDING BEHIND THIS TREE, CHARLIE BROWN?
I'M JUST LOOKING AT THE HOUSE WHERE THE LITTLE RED-HAIRED GIRL LIVES..UNFORTUNATELY, SHE DOESN'T KNOW I'M ALIVE
WHAT YOU NEED THEN IS SOME SUBTLE WAY OF LETTING HER KNOW
I GUESS THAT'S RIGHT
HEY, KID, YOUR LOVER'S OUT HERE!
12-28
SCHULZ
© 1978 United Feature Syndicate, Inc.

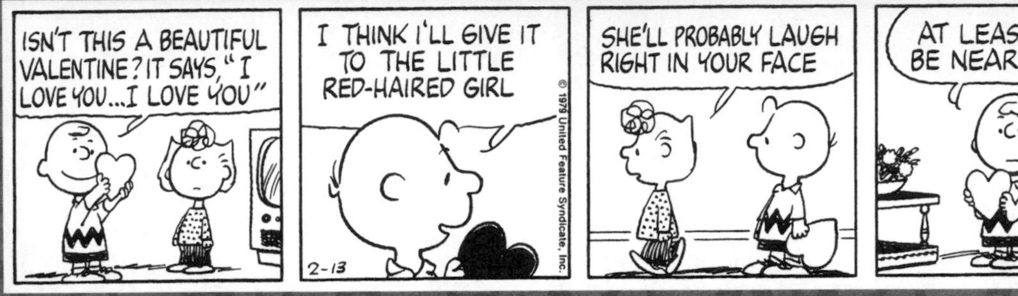

ISN'T THIS A BEAUTIFUL VALENTINE? IT SAYS, "I LOVE YOU...I LOVE YOU"
I THINK I'LL GIVE IT TO THE LITTLE RED-HAIRED GIRL
© 1979 United Feature Syndicate, Inc.
2-13
SHE'LL PROBABLY LAUGH RIGHT IN YOUR FACE
AT LEAST I'D BE NEAR HER!
SCHULZ

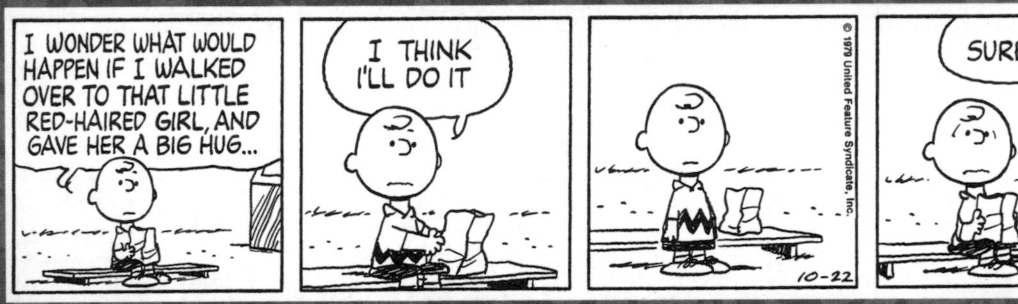

I WONDER WHAT WOULD HAPPEN IF I WALKED OVER TO THAT LITTLE RED-HAIRED GIRL, AND GAVE HER A BIG HUG...
I THINK I'LL DO IT
© 1979 United Feature Syndicate, Inc.
10-22
SURE
SCHULZ

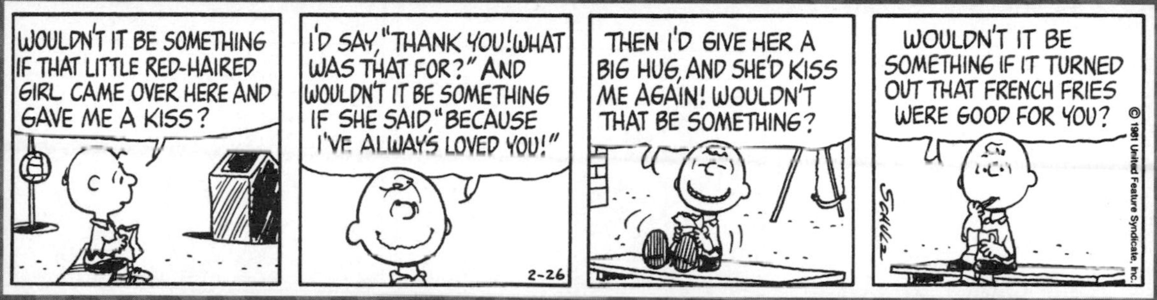
WOULDN'T IT BE SOMETHING IF THAT LITTLE RED-HAIRED GIRL CAME OVER HERE AND GAVE ME A KISS?
I'D SAY, "THANK YOU! WHAT WAS THAT FOR?" AND WOULDN'T IT BE SOMETHING IF SHE SAID, "BECAUSE I'VE ALWAYS LOVED YOU!"
2-26
THEN I'D GIVE HER A BIG HUG, AND SHE'D KISS ME AGAIN! WOULDN'T THAT BE SOMETHING?
WOULDN'T IT BE SOMETHING IF IT TURNED OUT THAT FRENCH FRIES WERE GOOD FOR YOU?
SCHULZ
© 1981 United Feature Syndicate, Inc.

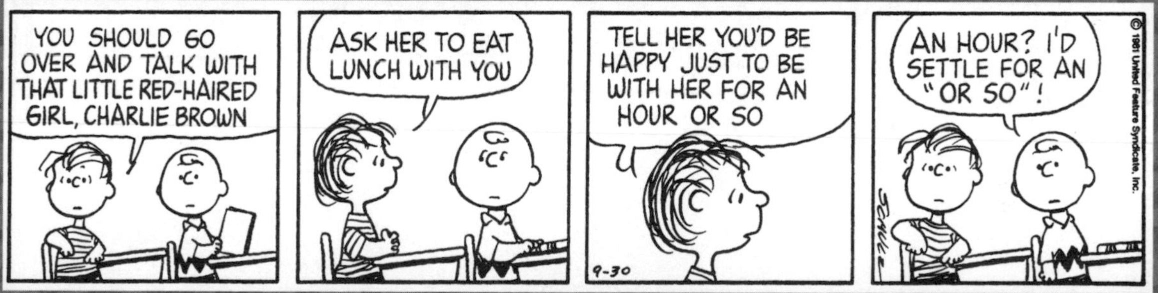
YOU SHOULD GO OVER AND TALK WITH THAT LITTLE RED-HAIRED GIRL, CHARLIE BROWN
ASK HER TO EAT LUNCH WITH YOU
TELL HER YOU'D BE HAPPY JUST TO BE WITH HER FOR AN HOUR OR SO
9-30
AN HOUR? I'D SETTLE FOR AN "OR SO"!
SCHULZ
© 1981 United Feature Syndicate, Inc.

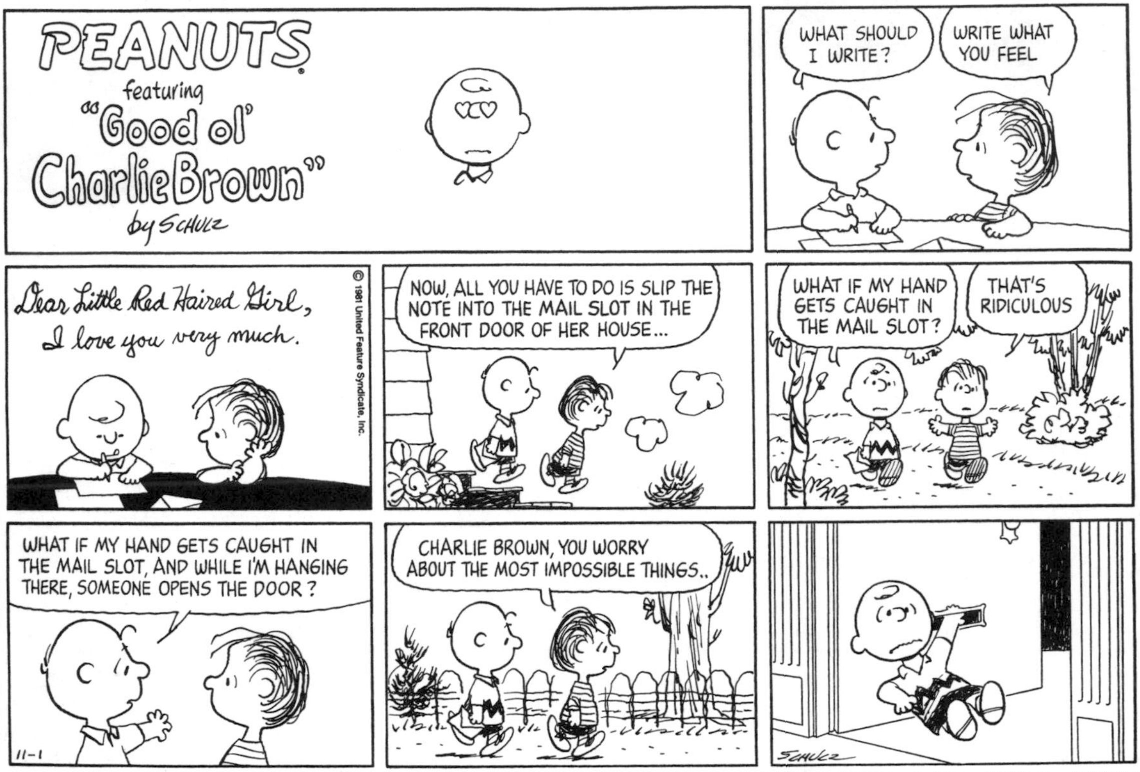
PEANUTS
featuring
"Good ol' CharlieBrown"
by SCHULZ
WHAT SHOULD I WRITE?
WRITE WHAT YOU FEEL
Dear Little Red Haired Girl,
I love you very much.
© 1981 United Feature Syndicate, Inc.
NOW, ALL YOU HAVE TO DO IS SLIP THE NOTE INTO THE MAIL SLOT IN THE FRONT DOOR OF HER HOUSE...
WHAT IF MY HAND GETS CAUGHT IN THE MAIL SLOT?
THAT'S RIDICULOUS
WHAT IF MY HAND GETS CAUGHT IN THE MAIL SLOT, AND WHILE I'M HANGING THERE, SOMEONE OPENS THE DOOR?
11-1
CHARLIE BROWN, YOU WORRY ABOUT THE MOST IMPOSSIBLE THINGS..
SCHULZ

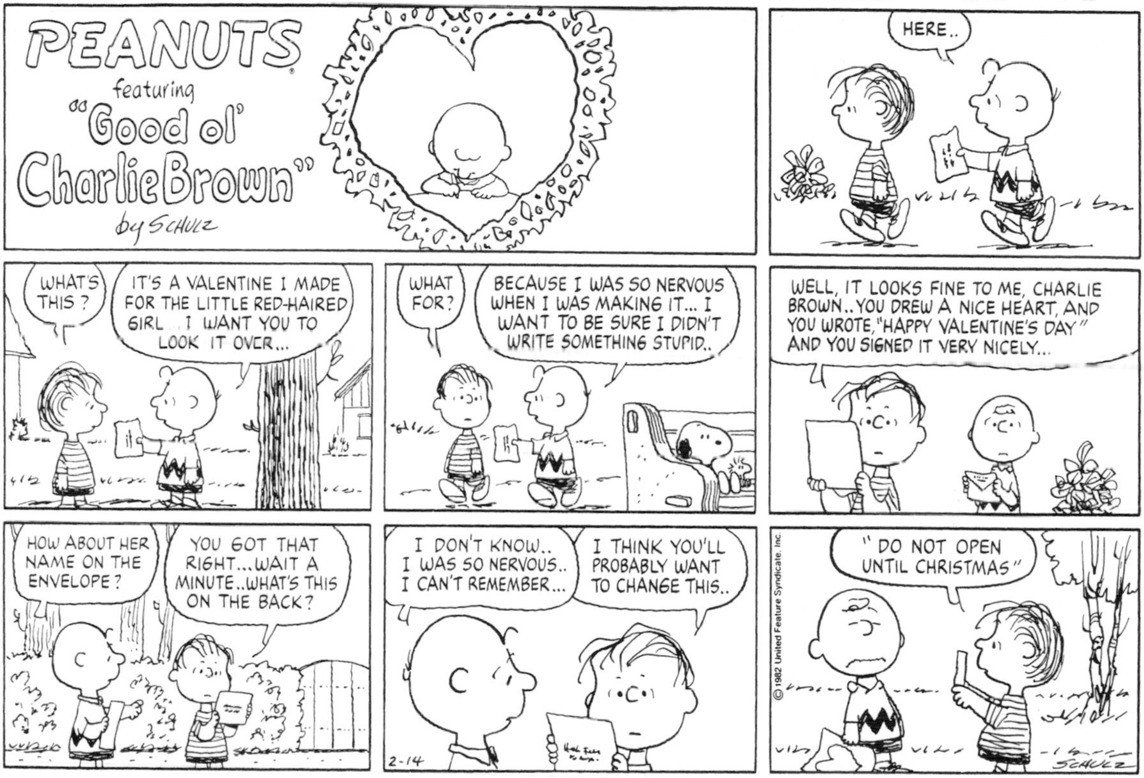
PEANUTS
featuring
"Good ol' CharlieBrown"
by SCHULZ
HERE..
WHAT'S THIS?
IT'S A VALENTINE I MADE FOR THE LITTLE RED-HAIRED GIRL... I WANT YOU TO LOOK IT OVER...
WHAT FOR?
BECAUSE I WAS SO NERVOUS WHEN I WAS MAKING IT... I WANT TO BE SURE I DIDN'T WRITE SOMETHING STUPID..
WELL, IT LOOKS FINE TO ME, CHARLIE BROWN..YOU DREW A NICE HEART, AND YOU WROTE, "HAPPY VALENTINE'S DAY" AND YOU SIGNED IT VERY NICELY...
HOW ABOUT HER NAME ON THE ENVELOPE?
YOU GOT THAT RIGHT...WAIT A MINUTE..WHAT'S THIS ON THE BACK?
I DON'T KNOW.. I WAS SO NERVOUS.. I CAN'T REMEMBER...
I THINK YOU'LL PROBABLY WANT TO CHANGE THIS..
2-14
"DO NOT OPEN UNTIL CHRISTMAS"
© 1982 United Feature Syndicate, Inc.
SCHULZ

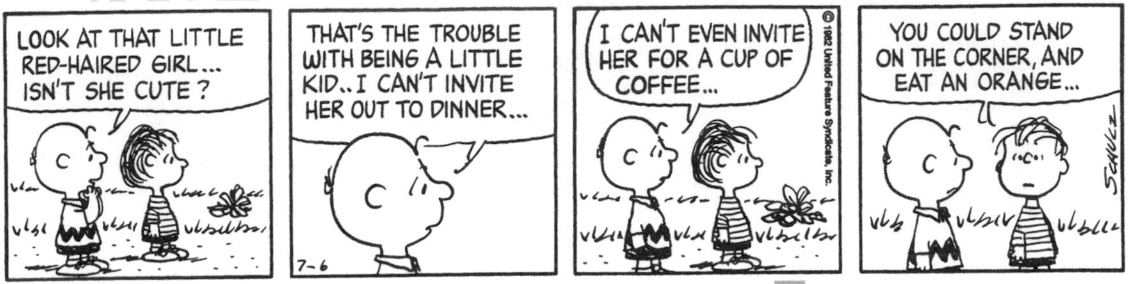
LOOK AT THAT LITTLE RED-HAIRED GIRL... ISN'T SHE CUTE?
THAT'S THE TROUBLE WITH BEING A LITTLE KID.. I CAN'T INVITE HER OUT TO DINNER...
7-6
I CAN'T EVEN INVITE HER FOR A CUP OF COFFEE...
© 1982 United Feature Syndicate, Inc.
YOU COULD STAND ON THE CORNER, AND EAT AN ORANGE...
SCHULZ

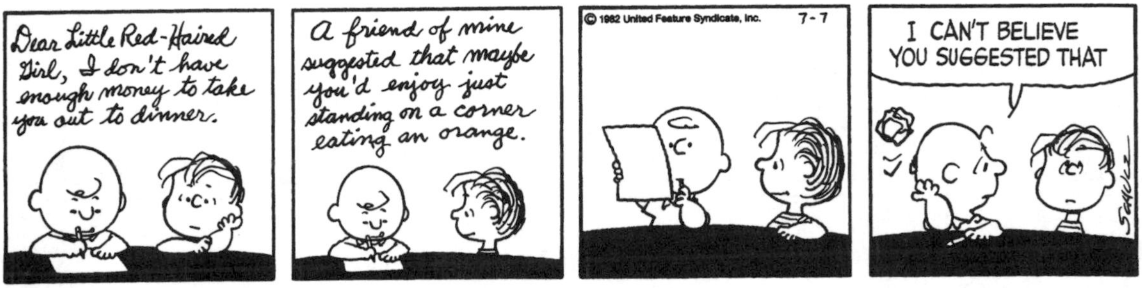
Dear Little Red-Haired Girl, I don't have enough money to take you out to dinner.
A friend of mine suggested that maybe you'd enjoy just standing on a corner eating an orange.
© 1982 United Feature Syndicate, Inc. 7-7
I CAN'T BELIEVE YOU SUGGESTED THAT
SCHULZ

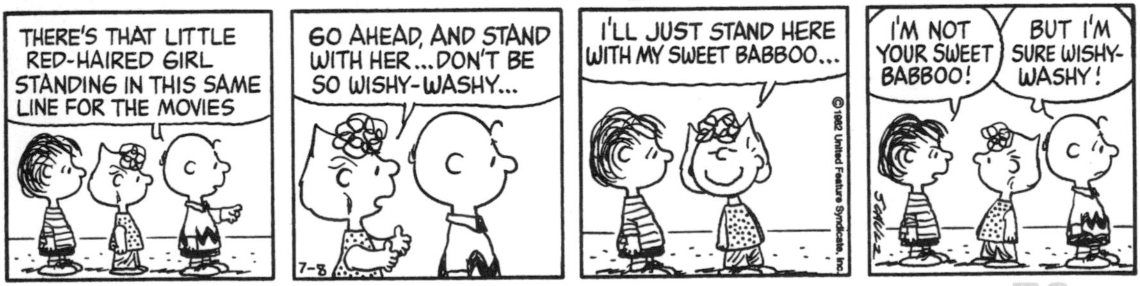
THERE'S THAT LITTLE RED-HAIRED GIRL STANDING IN THIS SAME LINE FOR THE MOVIES
GO AHEAD, AND STAND WITH HER... DON'T BE SO WISHY-WASHY...
7-8
I'LL JUST STAND HERE WITH MY SWEET BABBOO...
© 1982 United Feature Syndicate, Inc.
I'M NOT YOUR SWEET BABBOO!
BUT I'M SURE WISHY-WASHY!
SCHULZ

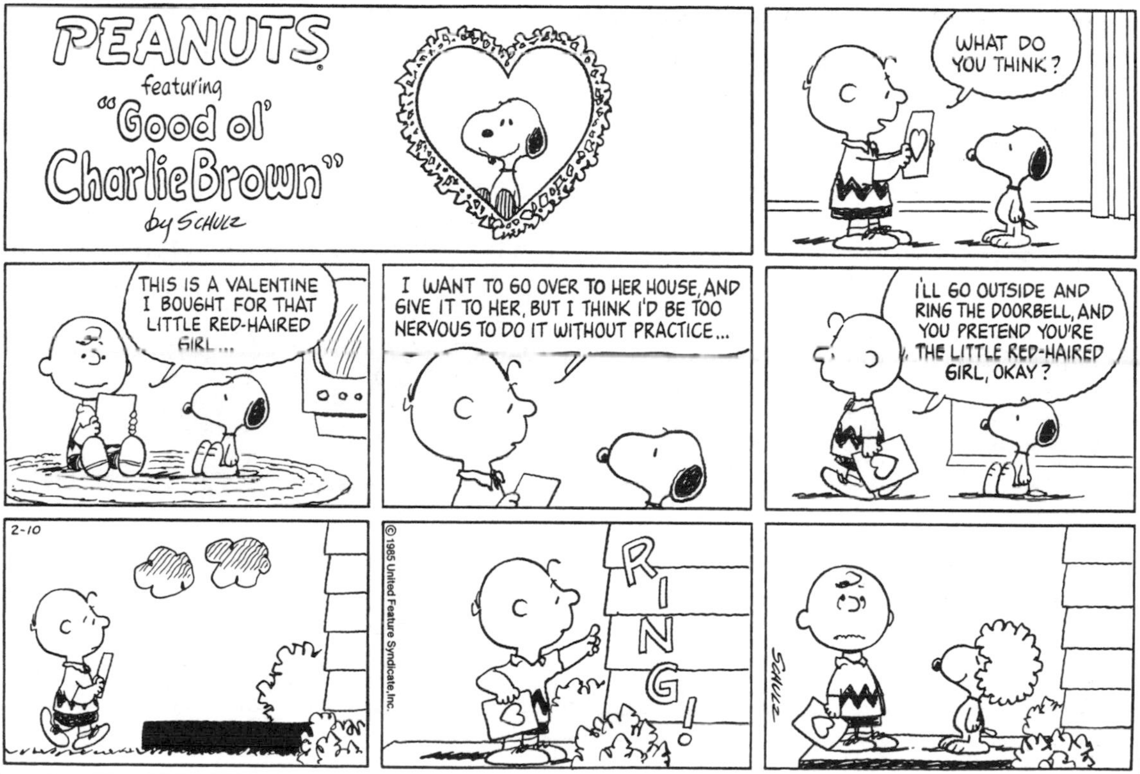
PEANUTS
featuring
"Good ol' Charlie Brown"
by SCHULZ
WHAT DO YOU THINK?
THIS IS A VALENTINE I BOUGHT FOR THAT LITTLE RED-HAIRED GIRL...
I WANT TO GO OVER TO HER HOUSE, AND GIVE IT TO HER, BUT I THINK I'D BE TOO NERVOUS TO DO IT WITHOUT PRACTICE...
I'LL GO OUTSIDE AND RING THE DOORBELL, AND YOU PRETEND YOU'RE THE LITTLE RED-HAIRED GIRL, OKAY?
2-10
© 1985 United Feature Syndicate, Inc.
RING!
SCHULZ

I DREAMED ABOUT THAT LITTLE RED HAIRED GIRL AGAIN LAST NIGHT...
NOW, I'LL BE THINKING ABOUT HER ALL DAY, AND BE DEPRESSED...
© 1985 United Feature Syndicate, Inc.
I THINK I KNOW HOW YOU FEEL, CHARLIE BROWN.. YOU'D LIKE TO CRY, BUT YOU'RE TOO MACHO..
9-27
I **AM** ?!
SCHULZ

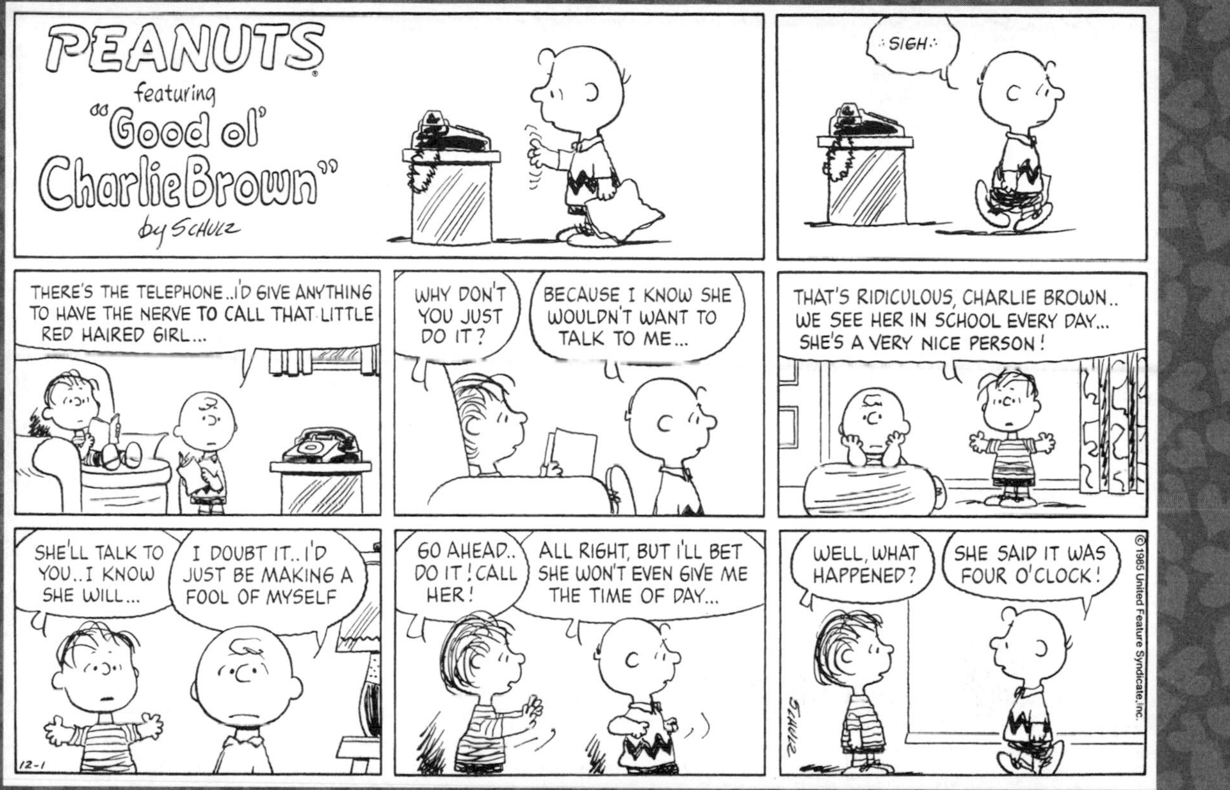
PEANUTS
featuring
"Good ol' CharlieBrown"
by SCHULZ
:: SIGH ::
THERE'S THE TELEPHONE..I'D GIVE ANYTHING TO HAVE THE NERVE TO CALL THAT LITTLE RED HAIRED GIRL...
WHY DON'T YOU JUST DO IT?
BECAUSE I KNOW SHE WOULDN'T WANT TO TALK TO ME...
THAT'S RIDICULOUS, CHARLIE BROWN.. WE SEE HER IN SCHOOL EVERY DAY... SHE'S A VERY NICE PERSON!
SHE'LL TALK TO YOU..I KNOW SHE WILL...
I DOUBT IT..I'D JUST BE MAKING A FOOL OF MYSELF
12-1
GO AHEAD.. DO IT! CALL HER!
ALL RIGHT, BUT I'LL BET SHE WON'T EVEN GIVE ME THE TIME OF DAY...
WELL, WHAT HAPPENED?
SHE SAID IT WAS FOUR O'CLOCK!
SCHULZ
© 1985 United Feature Syndicate, Inc.

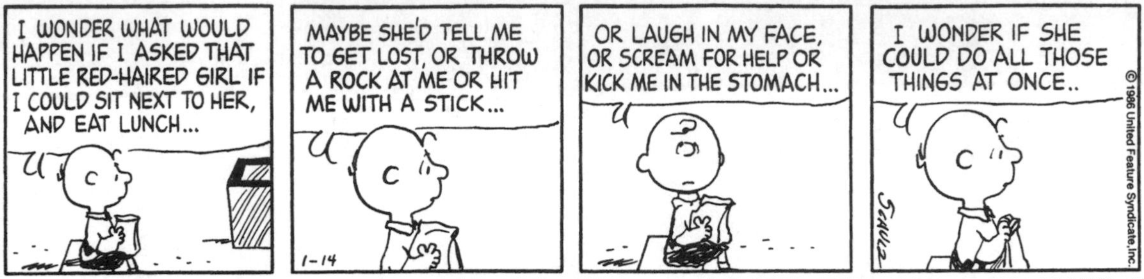
I WONDER WHAT WOULD HAPPEN IF I ASKED THAT LITTLE RED-HAIRED GIRL IF I COULD SIT NEXT TO HER, AND EAT LUNCH...
MAYBE SHE'D TELL ME TO GET LOST, OR THROW A ROCK AT ME OR HIT ME WITH A STICK...
1-14
OR LAUGH IN MY FACE, OR SCREAM FOR HELP OR KICK ME IN THE STOMACH...
I WONDER IF SHE COULD DO ALL THOSE THINGS AT ONCE..
SCHULZ
© 1986 United Feature Syndicate, Inc.

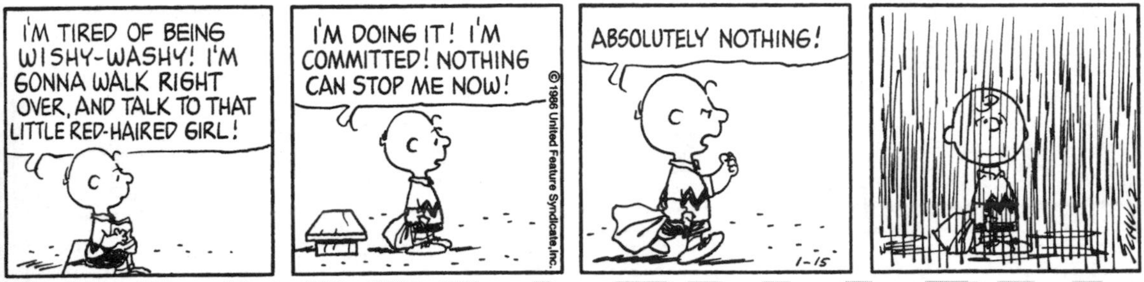
I'M TIRED OF BEING WISHY-WASHY! I'M GONNA WALK RIGHT OVER, AND TALK TO THAT LITTLE RED-HAIRED GIRL!
I'M DOING IT! I'M COMMITTED! NOTHING CAN STOP ME NOW!
© 1986 United Feature Syndicate, Inc.
ABSOLUTELY NOTHING!
1-15
SCHULZ

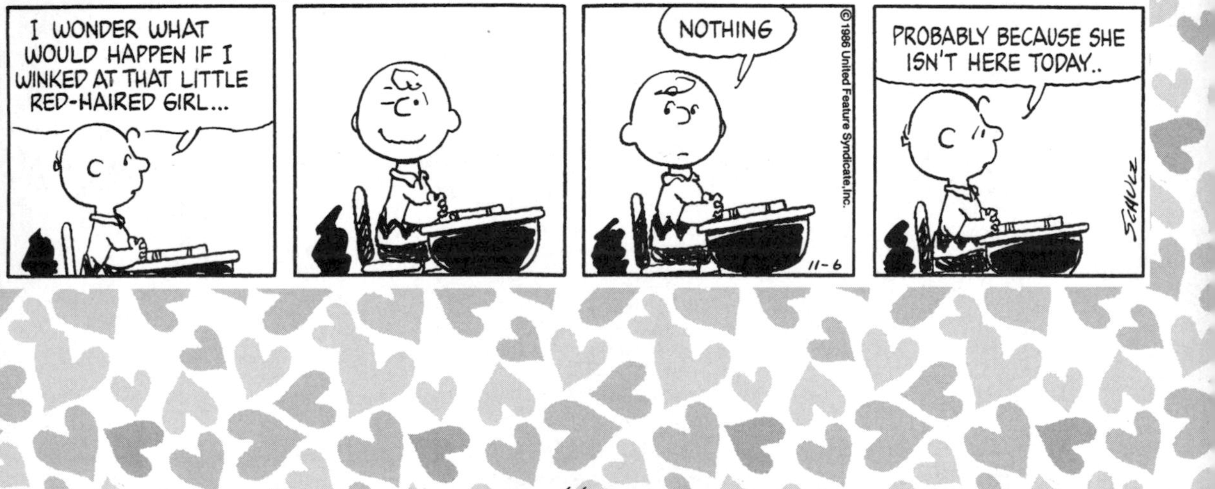
I WONDER WHAT WOULD HAPPEN IF I WINKED AT THAT LITTLE RED-HAIRED GIRL...
NOTHING
11-6
© 1986 United Feature Syndicate, Inc.
PROBABLY BECAUSE SHE ISN'T HERE TODAY..
SCHULZ

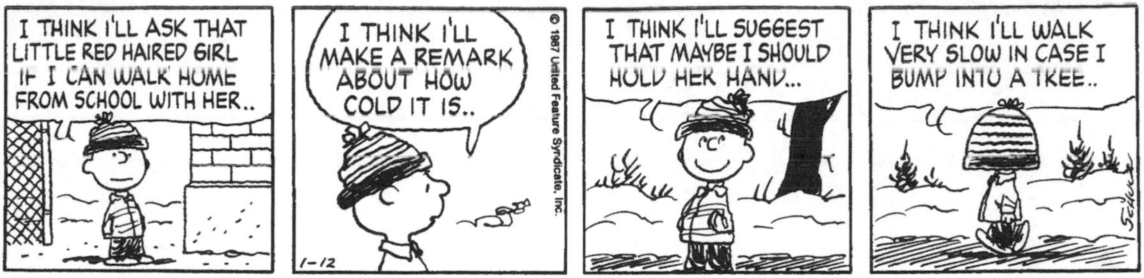
I THINK I'LL ASK THAT LITTLE RED HAIRED GIRL IF I CAN WALK HOME FROM SCHOOL WITH HER..
I THINK I'LL MAKE A REMARK ABOUT HOW COLD IT IS..
© 1987 United Feature Syndicate, Inc.
1-12
I THINK I'LL SUGGEST THAT MAYBE I SHOULD HOLD HER HAND...
I THINK I'LL WALK VERY SLOW IN CASE I BUMP INTO A TREE..
SCHULZ

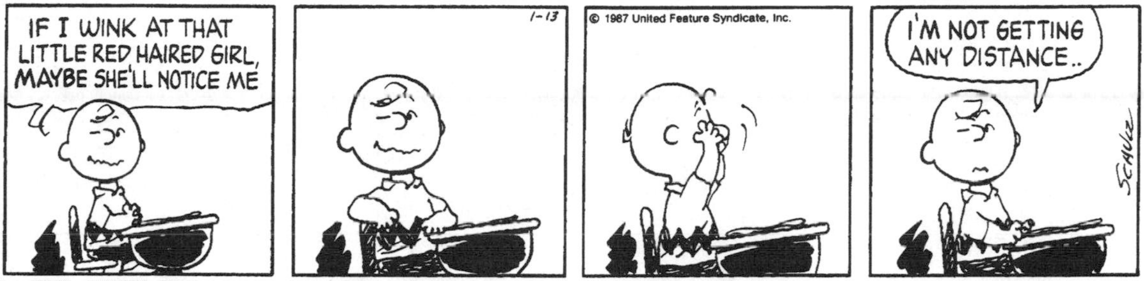
IF I WINK AT THAT LITTLE RED HAIRED GIRL, MAYBE SHE'LL NOTICE ME
1-13
© 1987 United Feature Syndicate, Inc.
I'M NOT GETTING ANY DISTANCE..
SCHULZ

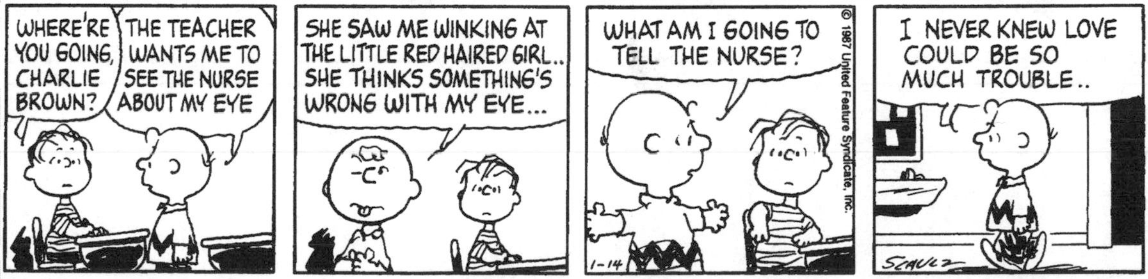
WHERE'RE YOU GOING, CHARLIE BROWN?
THE TEACHER WANTS ME TO SEE THE NURSE ABOUT MY EYE
SHE SAW ME WINKING AT THE LITTLE RED HAIRED GIRL.. SHE THINKS SOMETHING'S WRONG WITH MY EYE...
WHAT AM I GOING TO TELL THE NURSE?
© 1987 United Feature Syndicate, Inc.
1-14
I NEVER KNEW LOVE COULD BE SO MUCH TROUBLE..
SCHULZ

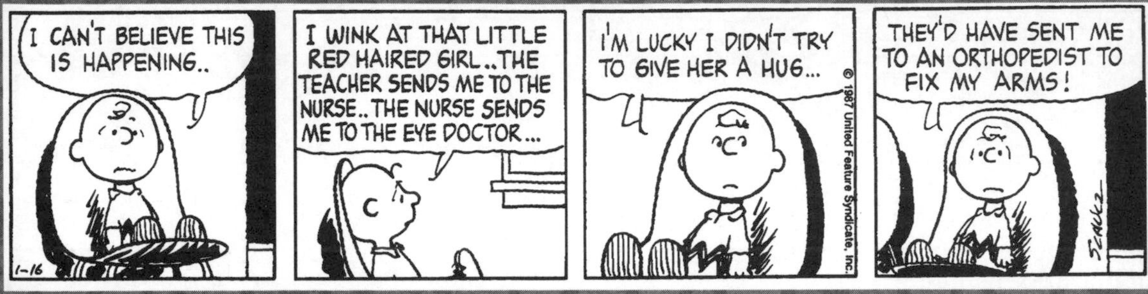
I CAN'T BELIEVE THIS IS HAPPENING..
I WINK AT THAT LITTLE RED HAIRED GIRL..THE TEACHER SENDS ME TO THE NURSE..THE NURSE SENDS ME TO THE EYE DOCTOR...
I'M LUCKY I DIDN'T TRY TO GIVE HER A HUG...
THEY'D HAVE SENT ME TO AN ORTHOPEDIST TO FIX MY ARMS!
1-16
© 1987 United Feature Syndicate, Inc.
SCHULZ

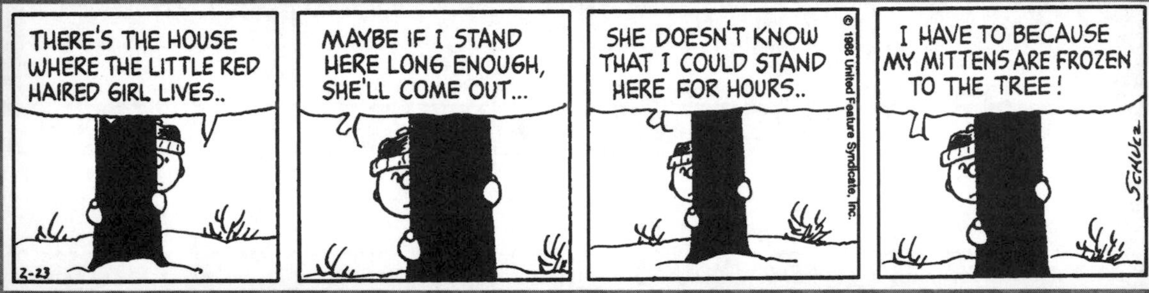
THERE'S THE HOUSE WHERE THE LITTLE RED HAIRED GIRL LIVES..
MAYBE IF I STAND HERE LONG ENOUGH, SHE'LL COME OUT...
SHE DOESN'T KNOW THAT I COULD STAND HERE FOR HOURS..
I HAVE TO BECAUSE MY MITTENS ARE FROZEN TO THE TREE!
2-23
© 1988 United Feature Syndicate, Inc.
SCHULZ

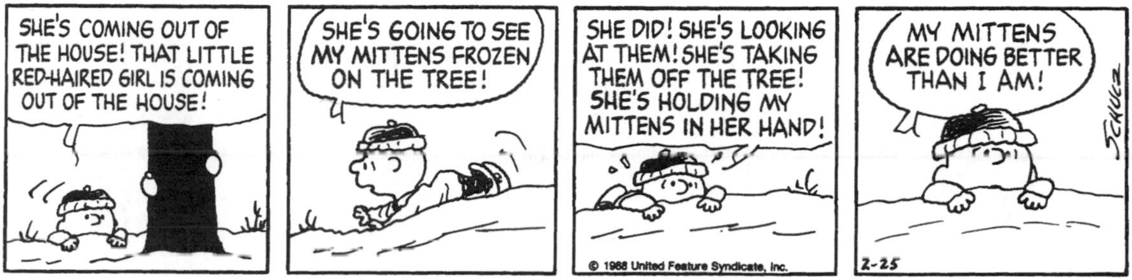
SHE'S COMING OUT OF THE HOUSE! THAT LITTLE RED-HAIRED GIRL IS COMING OUT OF THE HOUSE!
SHE'S GOING TO SEE MY MITTENS FROZEN ON THE TREE!
SHE DID! SHE'S LOOKING AT THEM! SHE'S TAKING THEM OFF THE TREE! SHE'S HOLDING MY MITTENS IN HER HAND!
MY MITTENS ARE DOING BETTER THAN I AM!
SCHULZ
© 1988 United Feature Syndicate, Inc.
2-25

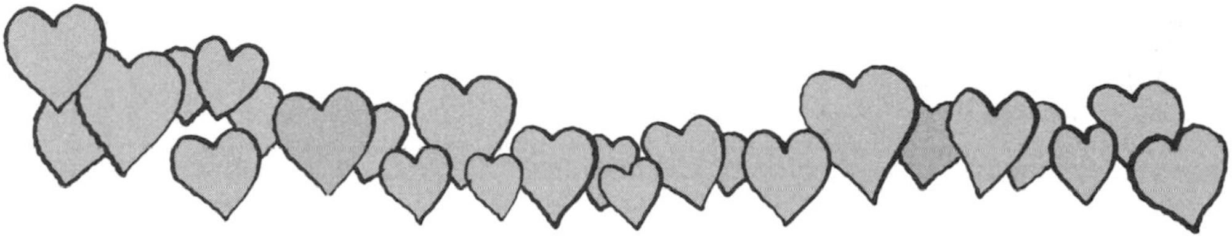

I'M AFRAID IF I GIVE THIS BOX OF CANDY TO THAT LITTLE RED HAIRED GIRL, SHE'LL JUST LAUGH IN MY FACE..

2-14

MAYBE I CAN HIDE BEHIND THIS TREE, AND WHEN SHE COMES BY, SHE'LL TAKE IT OUT OF MY HAND..

© 1989 United Feature Syndicate, Inc.

LOVE MAKES YOU DO STRANGE THINGS..

70

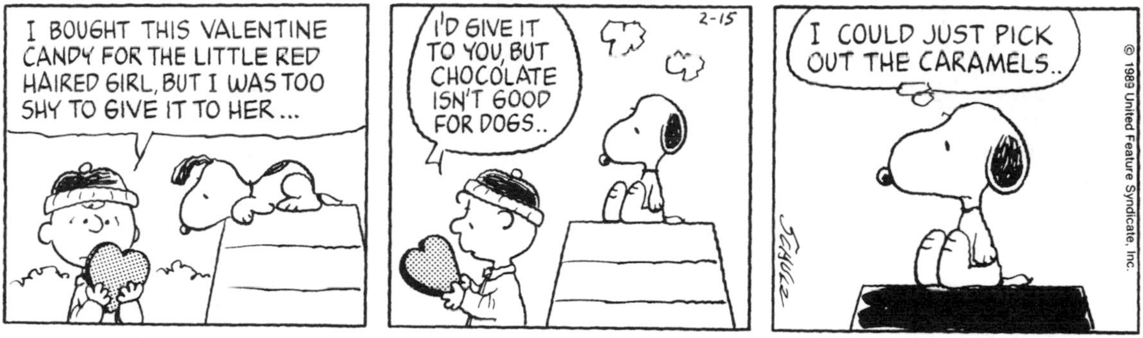
I BOUGHT THIS VALENTINE CANDY FOR THE LITTLE RED HAIRED GIRL, BUT I WAS TOO SHY TO GIVE IT TO HER...
I'D GIVE IT TO YOU, BUT CHOCOLATE ISN'T GOOD FOR DOGS..
2-15
I COULD JUST PICK OUT THE CARAMELS..
© 1989 United Feature Syndicate, Inc.

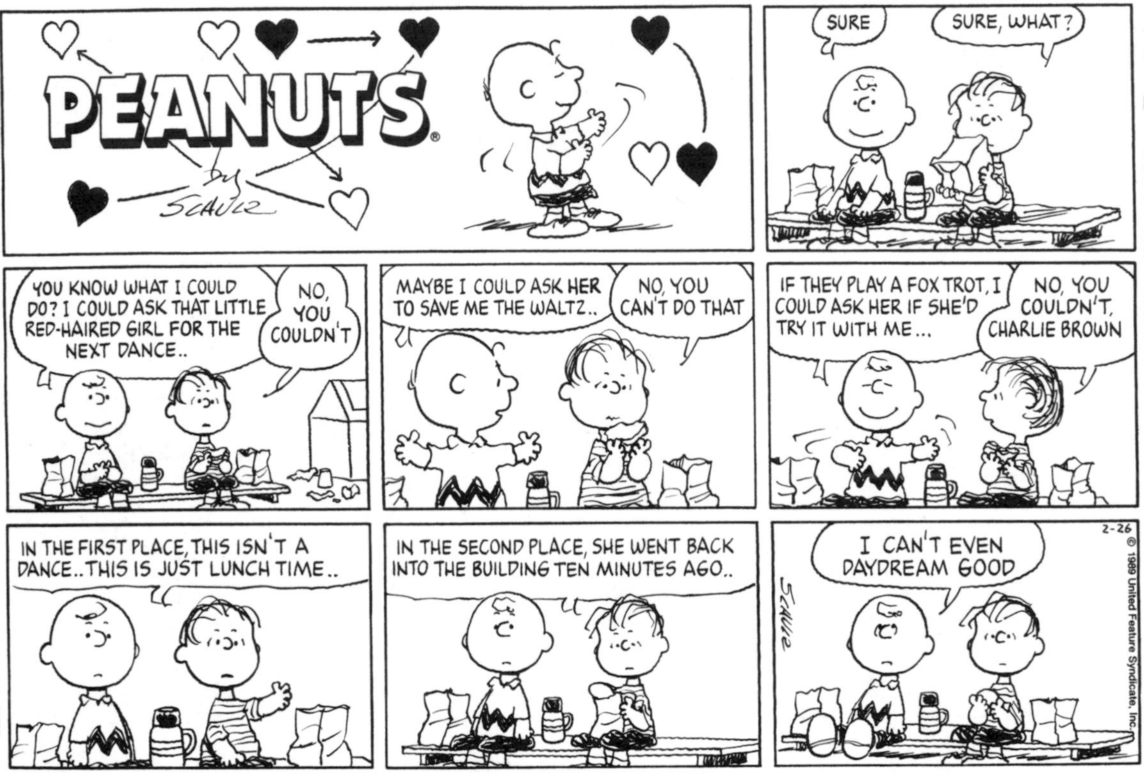
PEANUTS
by SCHULZ
SURE
SURE, WHAT?
YOU KNOW WHAT I COULD DO? I COULD ASK THAT LITTLE RED-HAIRED GIRL FOR THE NEXT DANCE..
NO, YOU COULDN'T
MAYBE I COULD ASK HER TO SAVE ME THE WALTZ..
NO, YOU CAN'T DO THAT
IF THEY PLAY A FOX TROT, I COULD ASK HER IF SHE'D TRY IT WITH ME...
NO, YOU COULDN'T, CHARLIE BROWN
IN THE FIRST PLACE, THIS ISN'T A DANCE..THIS IS JUST LUNCH TIME..
IN THE SECOND PLACE, SHE WENT BACK INTO THE BUILDING TEN MINUTES AGO..
2-26
© 1989 United Feature Syndicate, Inc.
SCHULZ
I CAN'T EVEN DAYDREAM GOOD

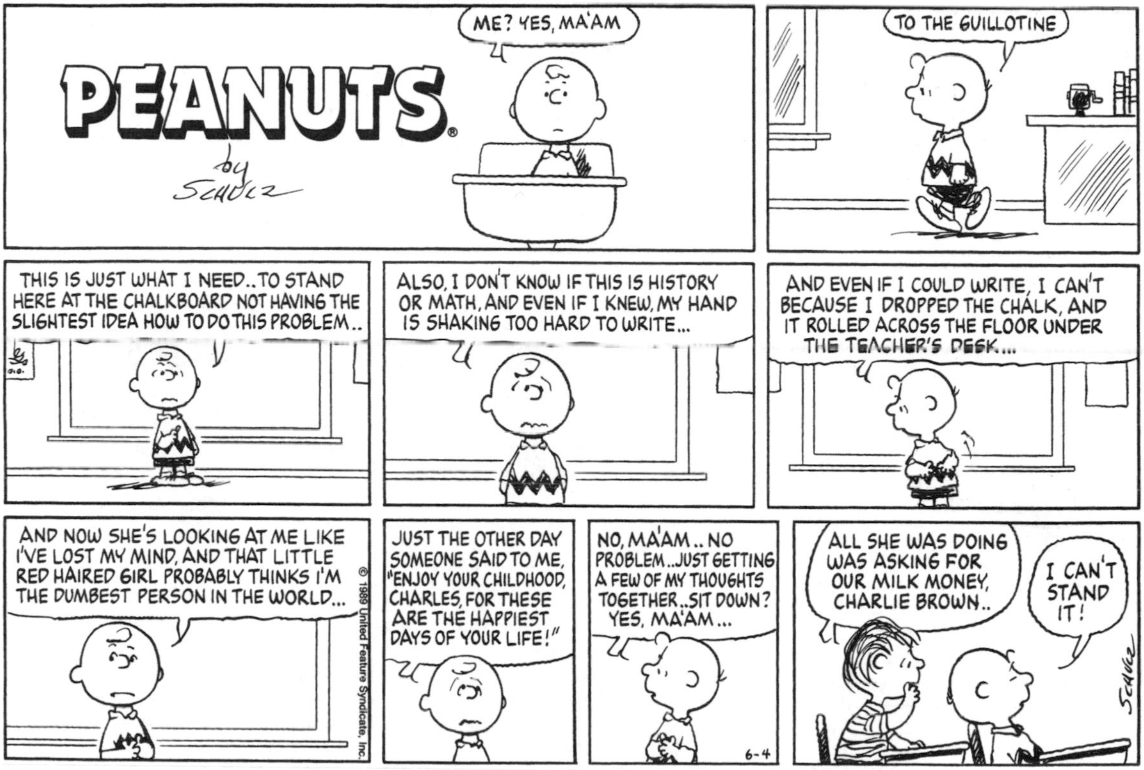
PEANUTS
by SCHULZ
ME? YES, MA'AM
TO THE GUILLOTINE
THIS IS JUST WHAT I NEED..TO STAND HERE AT THE CHALKBOARD NOT HAVING THE SLIGHTEST IDEA HOW TO DO THIS PROBLEM..
ALSO, I DON'T KNOW IF THIS IS HISTORY OR MATH, AND EVEN IF I KNEW, MY HAND IS SHAKING TOO HARD TO WRITE...
AND EVEN IF I COULD WRITE, I CAN'T BECAUSE I DROPPED THE CHALK, AND IT ROLLED ACROSS THE FLOOR UNDER THE TEACHER'S DESK...
AND NOW SHE'S LOOKING AT ME LIKE I'VE LOST MY MIND, AND THAT LITTLE RED HAIRED GIRL PROBABLY THINKS I'M THE DUMBEST PERSON IN THE WORLD...
© 1989 United Feature Syndicate, Inc.
JUST THE OTHER DAY SOMEONE SAID TO ME, "ENJOY YOUR CHILDHOOD, CHARLES, FOR THESE ARE THE HAPPIEST DAYS OF YOUR LIFE!"
NO, MA'AM.. NO PROBLEM...JUST GETTING A FEW OF MY THOUGHTS TOGETHER..SIT DOWN? YES, MA'AM...
6-4
ALL SHE WAS DOING WAS ASKING FOR OUR MILK MONEY, CHARLIE BROWN..
I CAN'T STAND IT!
SCHULZ

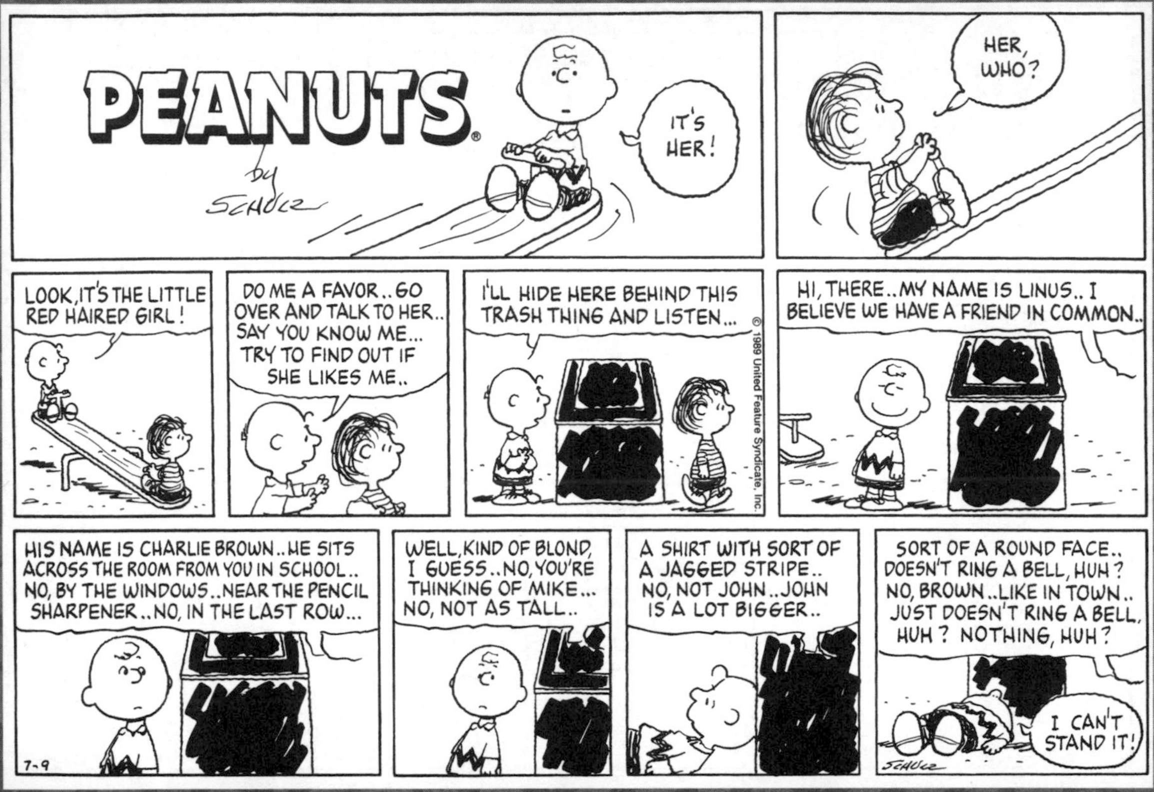
PEANUTS
by SCHULZ
IT'S HER!
HER, WHO?
LOOK, IT'S THE LITTLE RED HAIRED GIRL!
DO ME A FAVOR.. GO OVER AND TALK TO HER.. SAY YOU KNOW ME... TRY TO FIND OUT IF SHE LIKES ME..
I'LL HIDE HERE BEHIND THIS TRASH THING AND LISTEN...
© 1989 United Feature Syndicate, Inc.
HI, THERE.. MY NAME IS LINUS.. I BELIEVE WE HAVE A FRIEND IN COMMON..
HIS NAME IS CHARLIE BROWN.. HE SITS ACROSS THE ROOM FROM YOU IN SCHOOL.. NO, BY THE WINDOWS.. NEAR THE PENCIL SHARPENER.. NO, IN THE LAST ROW...
7-9
WELL, KIND OF BLOND, I GUESS.. NO, YOU'RE THINKING OF MIKE... NO, NOT AS TALL..
A SHIRT WITH SORT OF A JAGGED STRIPE.. NO, NOT JOHN.. JOHN IS A LOT BIGGER..
SORT OF A ROUND FACE.. DOESN'T RING A BELL, HUH? NO, BROWN.. LIKE IN TOWN.. JUST DOESN'T RING A BELL, HUH? NOTHING, HUH?
I CAN'T STAND IT!
SCHULZ

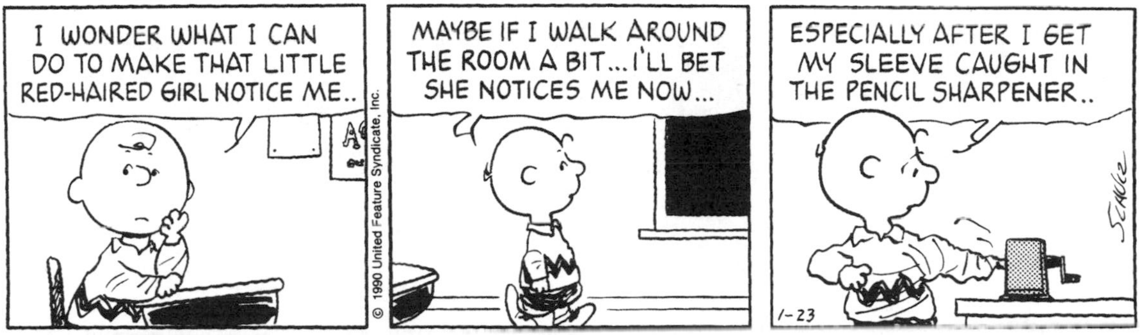
I WONDER WHAT I CAN DO TO MAKE THAT LITTLE RED-HAIRED GIRL NOTICE ME..
MAYBE IF I WALK AROUND THE ROOM A BIT... I'LL BET SHE NOTICES ME NOW...
ESPECIALLY AFTER I GET MY SLEEVE CAUGHT IN THE PENCIL SHARPENER..
© 1990 United Feature Syndicate, Inc.
1-23

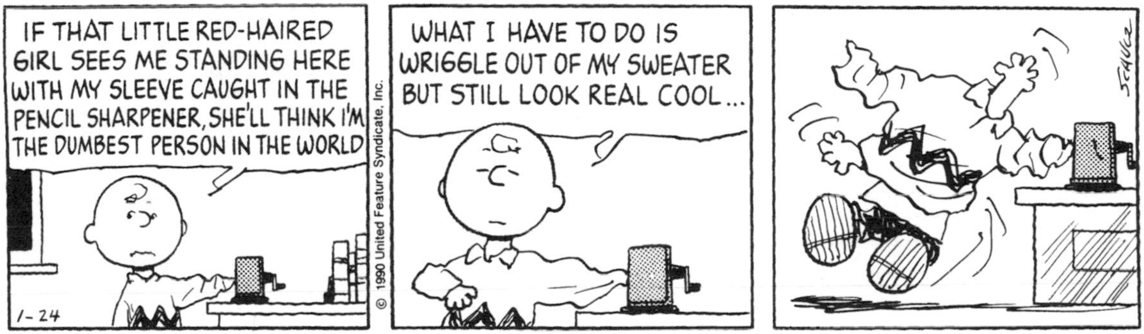
IF THAT LITTLE RED-HAIRED GIRL SEES ME STANDING HERE WITH MY SLEEVE CAUGHT IN THE PENCIL SHARPENER, SHE'LL THINK I'M THE DUMBEST PERSON IN THE WORLD
WHAT I HAVE TO DO IS WRIGGLE OUT OF MY SWEATER BUT STILL LOOK REAL COOL...
© 1990 United Feature Syndicate, Inc.
1-24

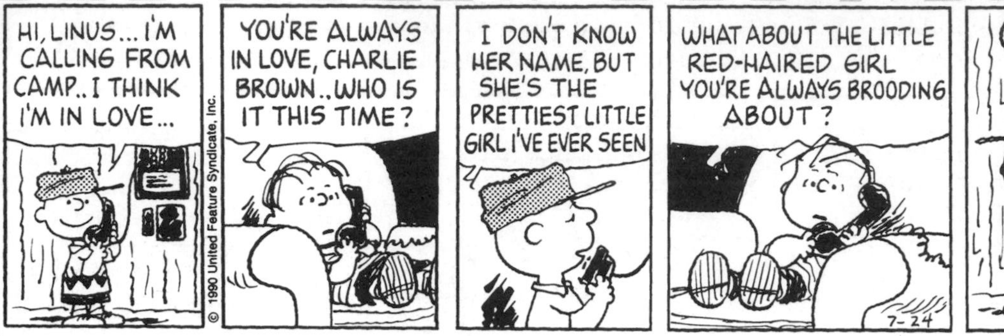
HI, LINUS... I'M CALLING FROM CAMP.. I THINK I'M IN LOVE...
© 1990 United Feature Syndicate, Inc.
YOU'RE ALWAYS IN LOVE, CHARLIE BROWN.. WHO IS IT THIS TIME?
I DON'T KNOW HER NAME, BUT SHE'S THE PRETTIEST LITTLE GIRL I'VE EVER SEEN
WHAT ABOUT THE LITTLE RED-HAIRED GIRL YOU'RE ALWAYS BROODING ABOUT?
7-24
WHO?

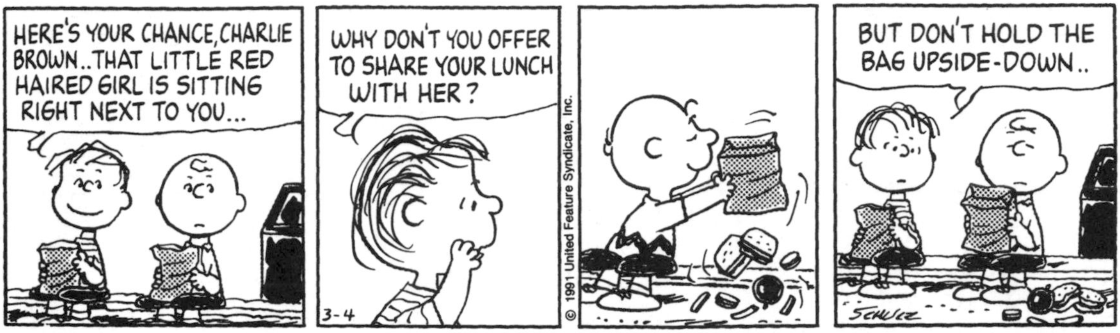
HERE'S YOUR CHANCE, CHARLIE BROWN.. THAT LITTLE RED HAIRED GIRL IS SITTING RIGHT NEXT TO YOU...
WHY DON'T YOU OFFER TO SHARE YOUR LUNCH WITH HER?
3-4
© 1991 United Feature Syndicate, Inc.
BUT DON'T HOLD THE BAG UPSIDE-DOWN..

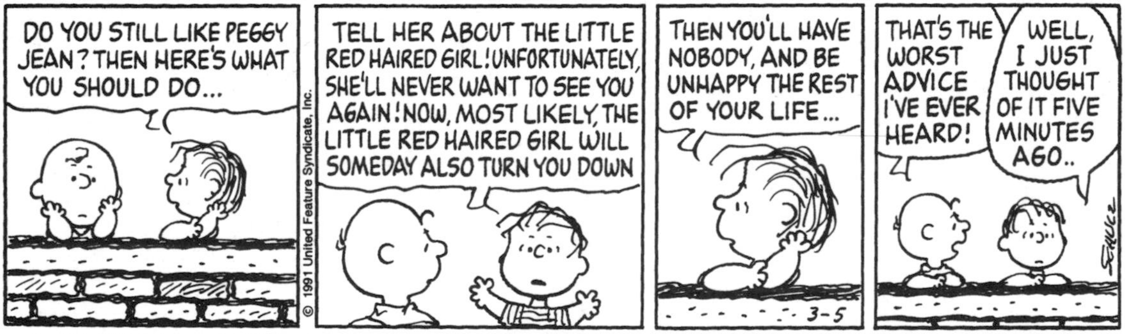
DO YOU STILL LIKE PEGGY JEAN? THEN HERE'S WHAT YOU SHOULD DO...
© 1991 United Feature Syndicate, Inc.
TELL HER ABOUT THE LITTLE RED HAIRED GIRL! UNFORTUNATELY, SHE'LL NEVER WANT TO SEE YOU AGAIN! NOW, MOST LIKELY, THE LITTLE RED HAIRED GIRL WILL SOMEDAY ALSO TURN YOU DOWN
THEN YOU'LL HAVE NOBODY, AND BE UNHAPPY THE REST OF YOUR LIFE...
3-5
THAT'S THE WORST ADVICE I'VE EVER HEARD!
WELL, I JUST THOUGHT OF IT FIVE MINUTES AGO..

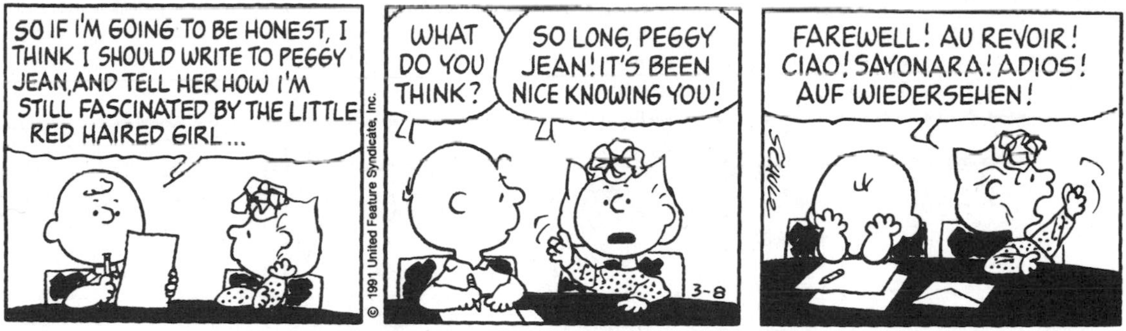
SO IF I'M GOING TO BE HONEST, I THINK I SHOULD WRITE TO PEGGY JEAN, AND TELL HER HOW I'M STILL FASCINATED BY THE LITTLE RED HAIRED GIRL...
WHAT DO YOU THINK?
SO LONG, PEGGY JEAN! IT'S BEEN NICE KNOWING YOU!
FAREWELL! AU REVOIR! CIAO! SAYONARA! ADIOS! AUF WIEDERSEHEN!
© 1991 United Feature Syndicate, Inc.
3-8
SCHULZ

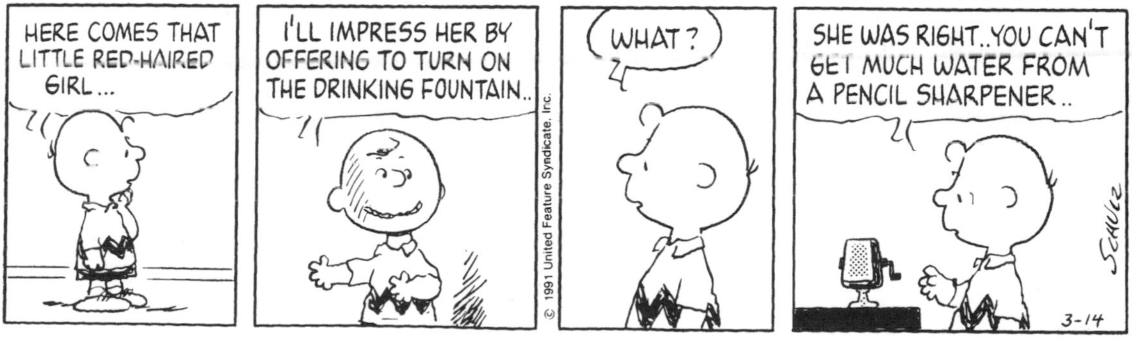
HERE COMES THAT LITTLE RED-HAIRED GIRL...
I'LL IMPRESS HER BY OFFERING TO TURN ON THE DRINKING FOUNTAIN..
WHAT?
SHE WAS RIGHT..YOU CAN'T GET MUCH WATER FROM A PENCIL SHARPENER..
© 1991 United Feature Syndicate, Inc.
SCHULZ
3-14

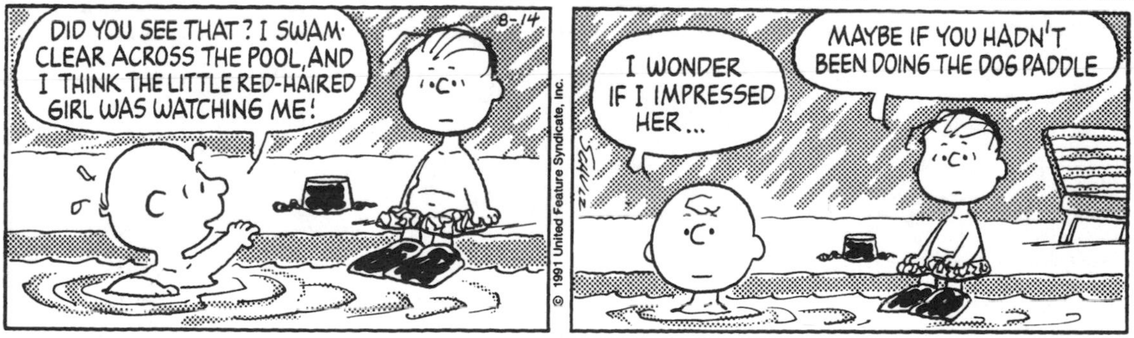
DID YOU SEE THAT? I SWAM CLEAR ACROSS THE POOL, AND I THINK THE LITTLE RED-HAIRED GIRL WAS WATCHING ME!
8-14
I WONDER IF I IMPRESSED HER...
MAYBE IF YOU HADN'T BEEN DOING THE DOG PADDLE
© 1991 United Feature Syndicate, Inc.
SCHULZ

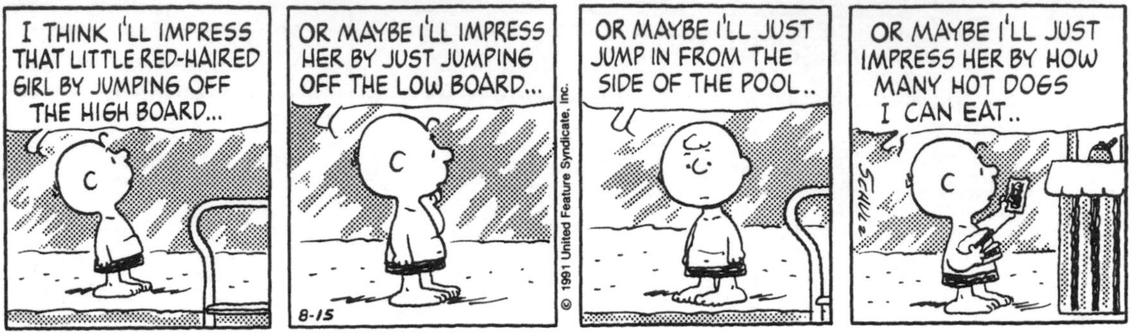
I THINK I'LL IMPRESS THAT LITTLE RED-HAIRED GIRL BY JUMPING OFF THE HIGH BOARD...
OR MAYBE I'LL IMPRESS HER BY JUST JUMPING OFF THE LOW BOARD...
8-15
© 1991 United Feature Syndicate, Inc.
OR MAYBE I'LL JUST JUMP IN FROM THE SIDE OF THE POOL..
OR MAYBE I'LL JUST IMPRESS HER BY HOW MANY HOT DOGS I CAN EAT..
SCHULZ

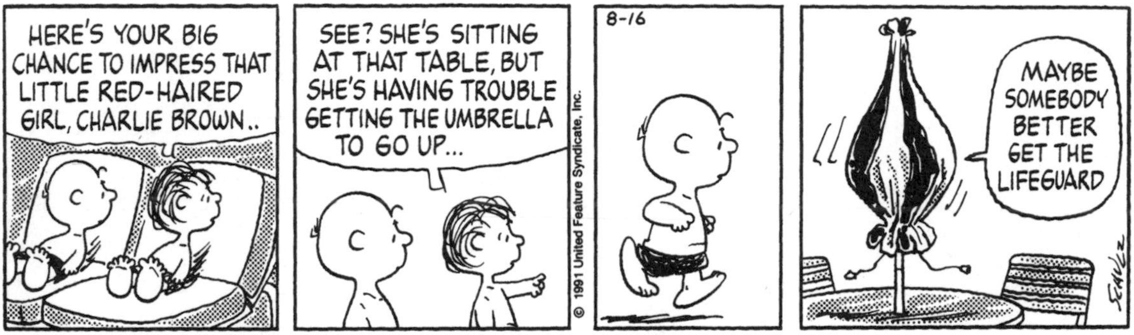
HERE'S YOUR BIG CHANCE TO IMPRESS THAT LITTLE RED-HAIRED GIRL, CHARLIE BROWN..
SEE? SHE'S SITTING AT THAT TABLE, BUT SHE'S HAVING TROUBLE GETTING THE UMBRELLA TO GO UP...
© 1991 United Feature Syndicate, Inc.
8-16
MAYBE SOMEBODY BETTER GET THE LIFEGUARD
SCHULZ

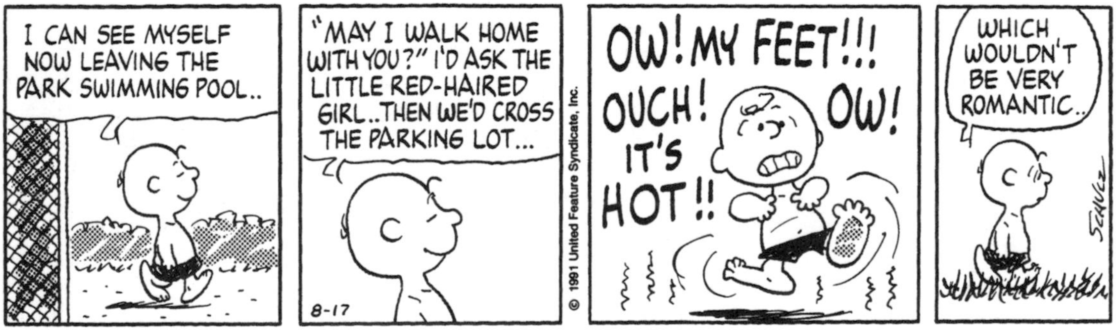
I CAN SEE MYSELF NOW LEAVING THE PARK SWIMMING POOL..
"MAY I WALK HOME WITH YOU?" I'D ASK THE LITTLE RED-HAIRED GIRL..THEN WE'D CROSS THE PARKING LOT...
8-17
© 1991 United Feature Syndicate, Inc.
OW! MY FEET!!!
OUCH! IT'S HOT!!
OW!
WHICH WOULDN'T BE VERY ROMANTIC..
SCHULZ

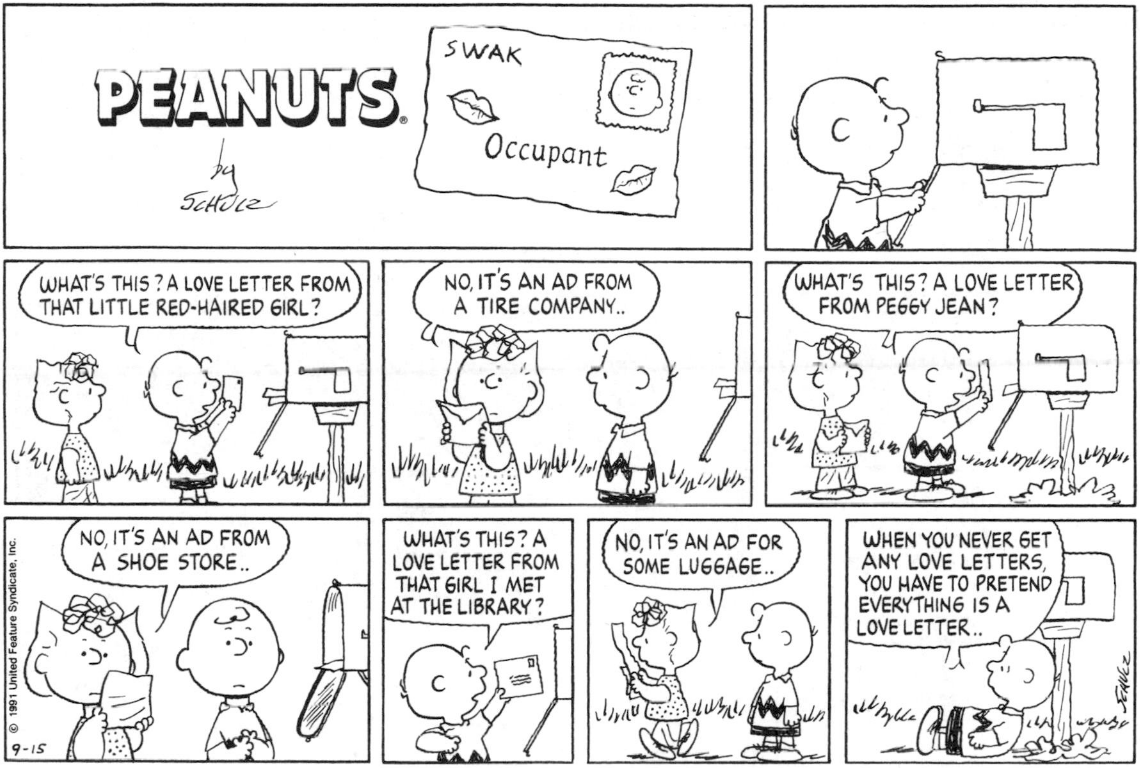
PEANUTS
by SCHULZ
SWAK
Occupant
WHAT'S THIS? A LOVE LETTER FROM THAT LITTLE RED-HAIRED GIRL?
NO, IT'S AN AD FROM A TIRE COMPANY..
WHAT'S THIS? A LOVE LETTER FROM PEGGY JEAN?
NO, IT'S AN AD FROM A SHOE STORE..
WHAT'S THIS? A LOVE LETTER FROM THAT GIRL I MET AT THE LIBRARY?
NO, IT'S AN AD FOR SOME LUGGAGE..
WHEN YOU NEVER GET ANY LOVE LETTERS, YOU HAVE TO PRETEND EVERYTHING IS A LOVE LETTER..
SCHULZ
© 1991 United Feature Syndicate, Inc.
9-15

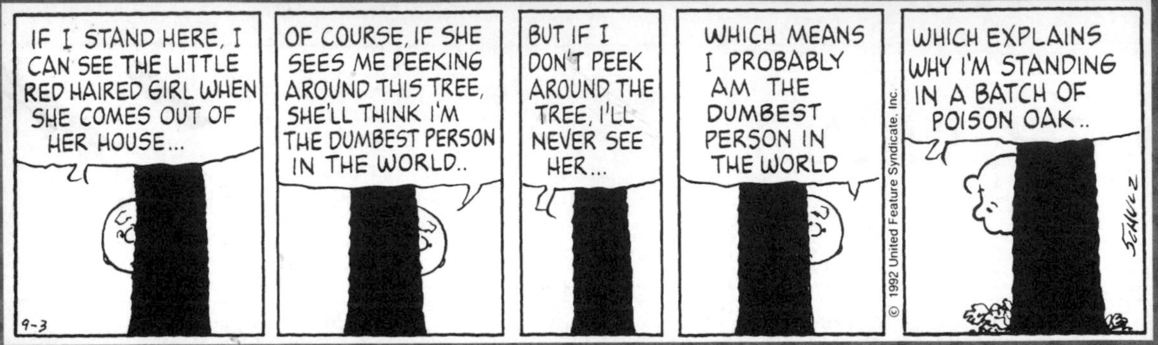
IF I STAND HERE, I CAN SEE THE LITTLE RED HAIRED GIRL WHEN SHE COMES OUT OF HER HOUSE...
OF COURSE, IF SHE SEES ME PEEKING AROUND THIS TREE, SHE'LL THINK I'M THE DUMBEST PERSON IN THE WORLD..
BUT IF I DON'T PEEK AROUND THE TREE, I'LL NEVER SEE HER...
WHICH MEANS I PROBABLY AM THE DUMBEST PERSON IN THE WORLD
WHICH EXPLAINS WHY I'M STANDING IN A BATCH OF POISON OAK..
9-3
© 1992 United Feature Syndicate, Inc.
SCHULZ

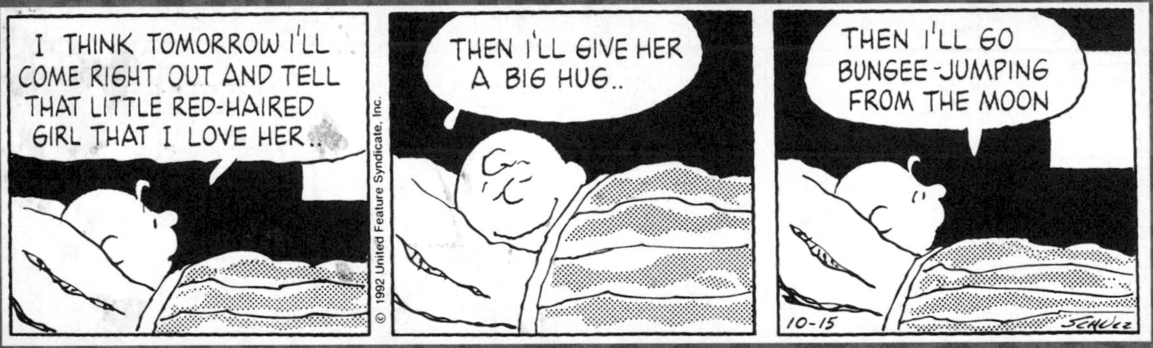
I THINK TOMORROW I'LL COME RIGHT OUT AND TELL THAT LITTLE RED-HAIRED GIRL THAT I LOVE HER..
THEN I'LL GIVE HER A BIG HUG..
THEN I'LL GO BUNGEE-JUMPING FROM THE MOON
© 1992 United Feature Syndicate, Inc.
10-15
SCHULZ

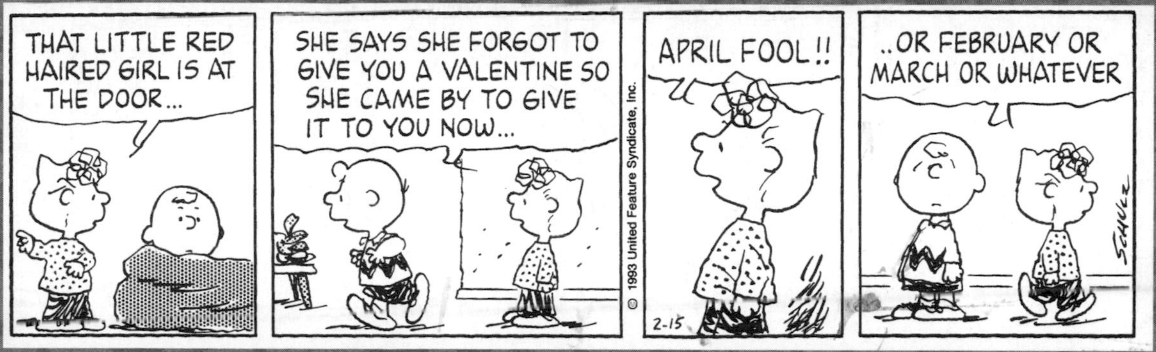
THAT LITTLE RED HAIRED GIRL IS AT THE DOOR...
SHE SAYS SHE FORGOT TO GIVE YOU A VALENTINE SO SHE CAME BY TO GIVE IT TO YOU NOW...
© 1993 United Feature Syndicate, Inc.
APRIL FOOL!!
2-15
..OR FEBRUARY OR MARCH OR WHATEVER
SCHULZ

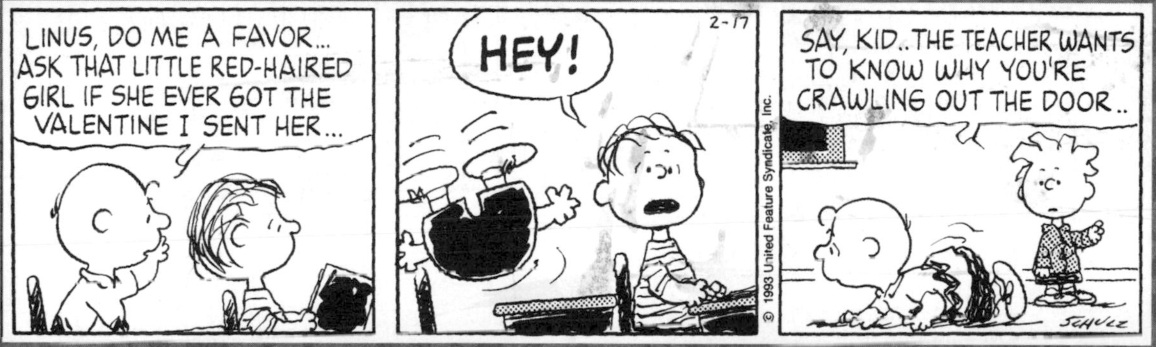
LINUS, DO ME A FAVOR... ASK THAT LITTLE RED-HAIRED GIRL IF SHE EVER GOT THE VALENTINE I SENT HER...
2-17
HEY!
© 1993 United Feature Syndicate, Inc.
SAY, KID..THE TEACHER WANTS TO KNOW WHY YOU'RE CRAWLING OUT THE DOOR..
SCHULZ

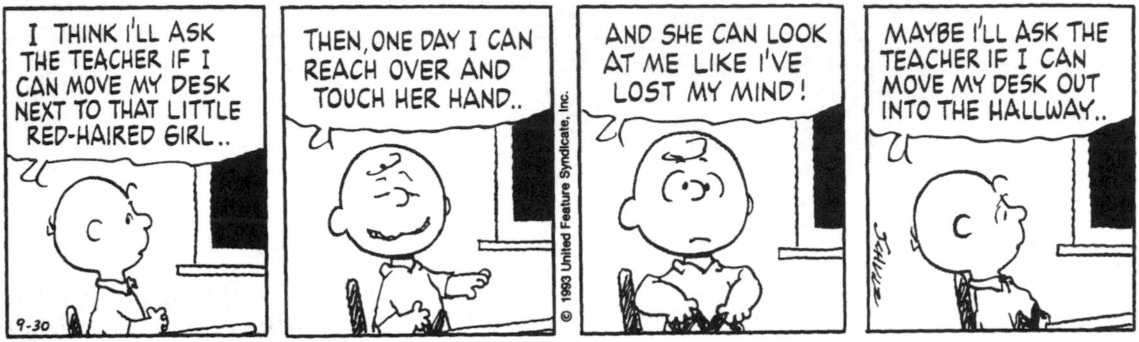
I THINK I'LL ASK THE TEACHER IF I CAN MOVE MY DESK NEXT TO THAT LITTLE RED-HAIRED GIRL..
THEN, ONE DAY I CAN REACH OVER AND TOUCH HER HAND..
AND SHE CAN LOOK AT ME LIKE I'VE LOST MY MIND!
MAYBE I'LL ASK THE TEACHER IF I CAN MOVE MY DESK OUT INTO THE HALLWAY..
9-30
© 1993 United Feature Syndicate, Inc.
SCHULZ

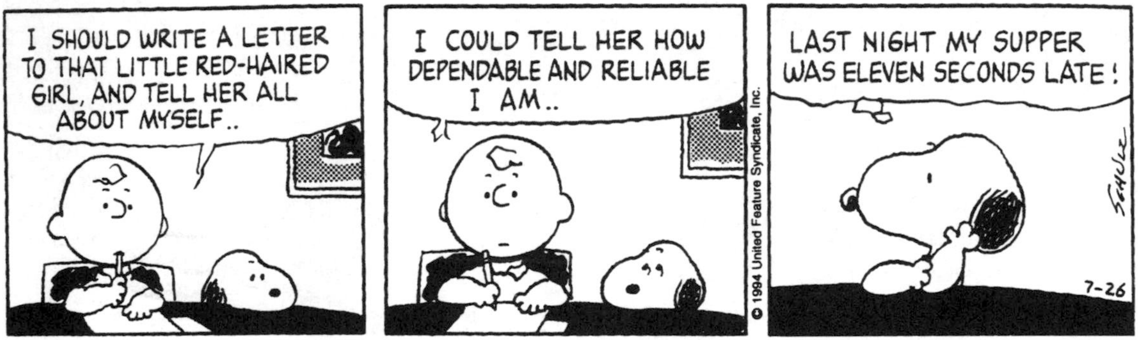
I SHOULD WRITE A LETTER TO THAT LITTLE RED-HAIRED GIRL, AND TELL HER ALL ABOUT MYSELF..
I COULD TELL HER HOW DEPENDABLE AND RELIABLE I AM..
LAST NIGHT MY SUPPER WAS ELEVEN SECONDS LATE!
© 1994 United Feature Syndicate, Inc.
SCHULZ
7-26

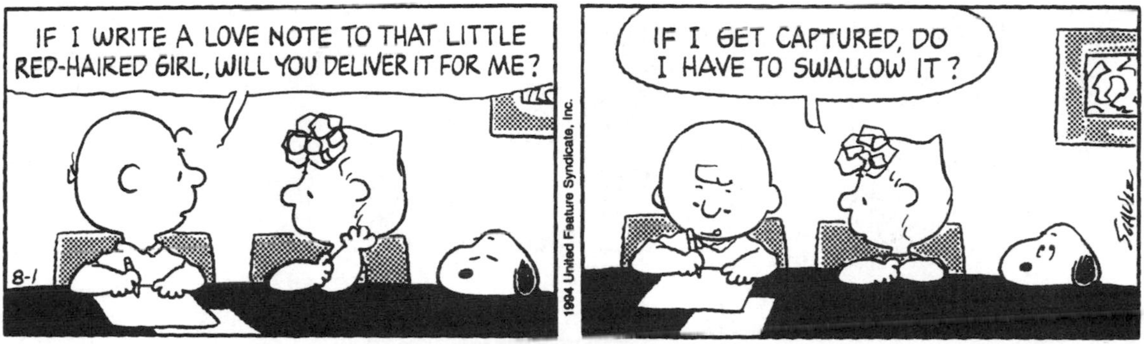
IF I WRITE A LOVE NOTE TO THAT LITTLE RED-HAIRED GIRL, WILL YOU DELIVER IT FOR ME?
8-1
1994 United Feature Syndicate, Inc.
IF I GET CAPTURED, DO I HAVE TO SWALLOW IT?
SCHULZ

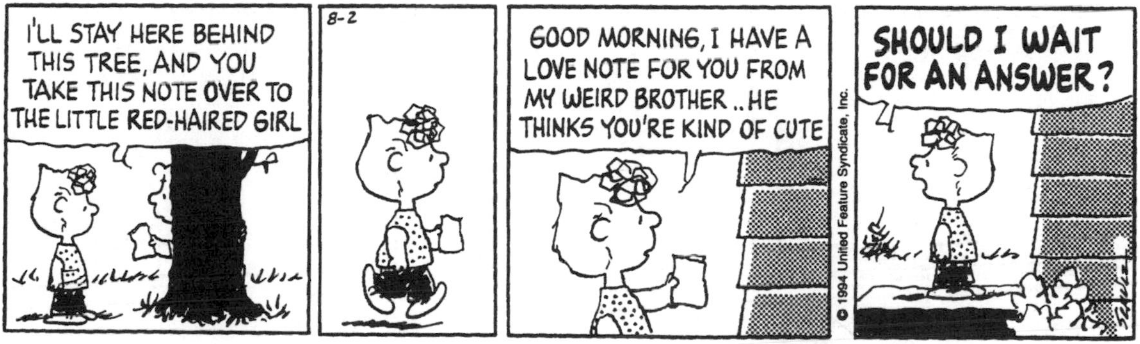
I'LL STAY HERE BEHIND THIS TREE, AND YOU TAKE THIS NOTE OVER TO THE LITTLE RED-HAIRED GIRL
8-2
GOOD MORNING, I HAVE A LOVE NOTE FOR YOU FROM MY WEIRD BROTHER .. HE THINKS YOU'RE KIND OF CUTE
© 1994 United Feature Syndicate, Inc.
SHOULD I WAIT FOR AN ANSWER?
SCHULZ

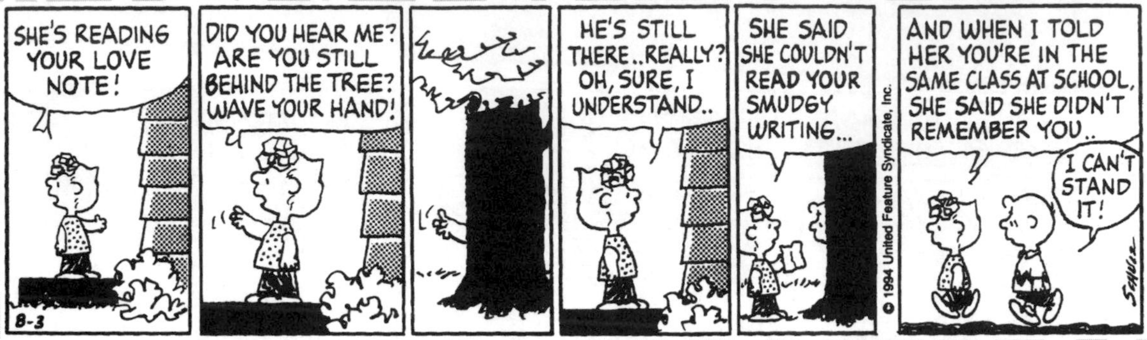
SHE'S READING YOUR LOVE NOTE!
8-3
DID YOU HEAR ME? ARE YOU STILL BEHIND THE TREE? WAVE YOUR HAND!
HE'S STILL THERE..REALLY? OH, SURE, I UNDERSTAND..
SHE SAID SHE COULDN'T READ YOUR SMUDGY WRITING...
© 1994 United Feature Syndicate, Inc.
AND WHEN I TOLD HER YOU'RE IN THE SAME CLASS AT SCHOOL, SHE SAID SHE DIDN'T REMEMBER YOU..
I CAN'T STAND IT!
SCHULZ

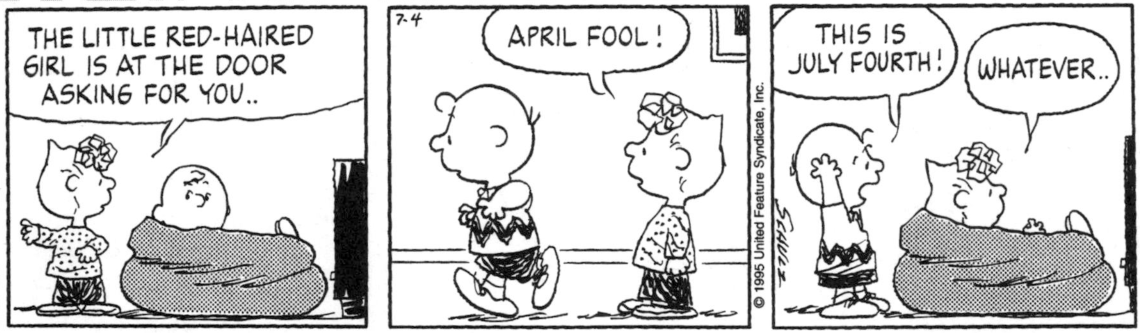
THE LITTLE RED-HAIRED GIRL IS AT THE DOOR ASKING FOR YOU..
7-4
APRIL FOOL!
© 1995 United Feature Syndicate, Inc.
SCHULZ
THIS IS JULY FOURTH!
WHATEVER..

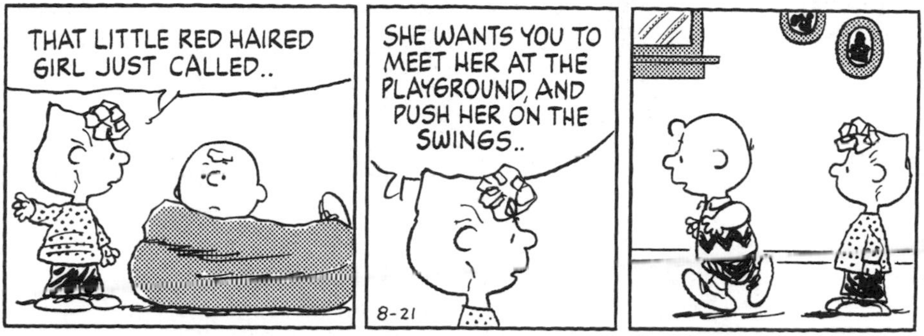
THAT LITTLE RED HAIRED GIRL JUST CALLED..
SHE WANTS YOU TO MEET HER AT THE PLAYGROUND, AND PUSH HER ON THE SWINGS..
8-21
© 1995 United Feature Syndicate, Inc.
AUGUST FOOL!
SCHULZ

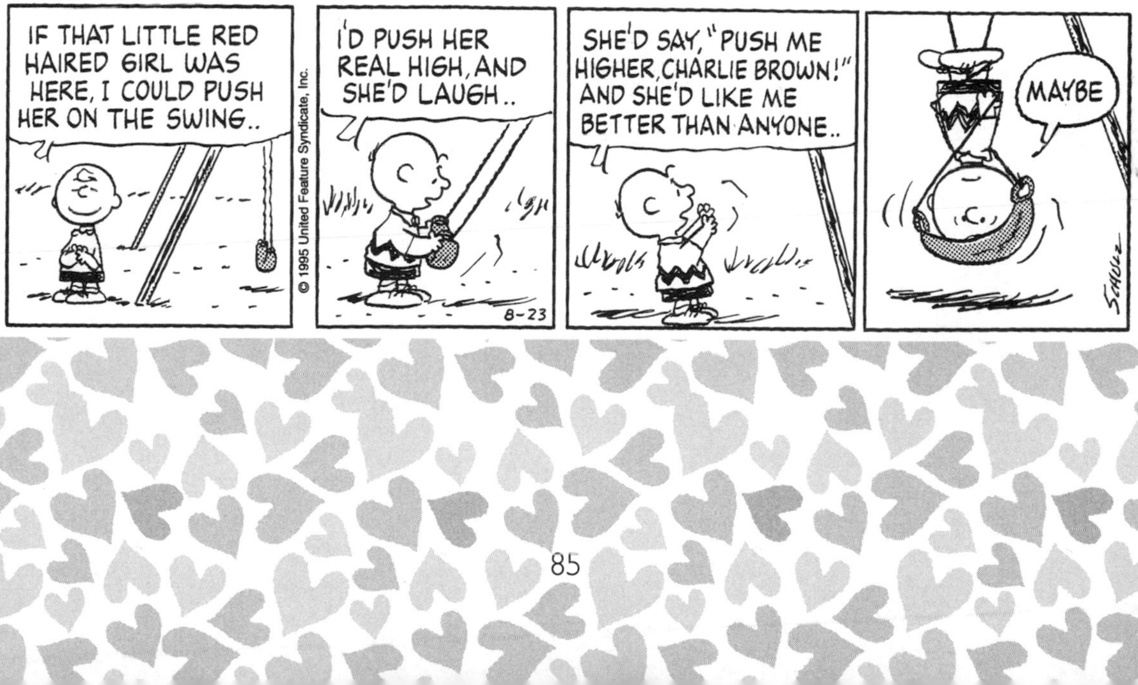
IF THAT LITTLE RED HAIRED GIRL WAS HERE, I COULD PUSH HER ON THE SWING..
© 1995 United Feature Syndicate, Inc.
I'D PUSH HER REAL HIGH, AND SHE'D LAUGH..
8-23
SHE'D SAY, "PUSH ME HIGHER, CHARLIE BROWN!" AND SHE'D LIKE ME BETTER THAN ANYONE..
MAYBE
SCHULZ

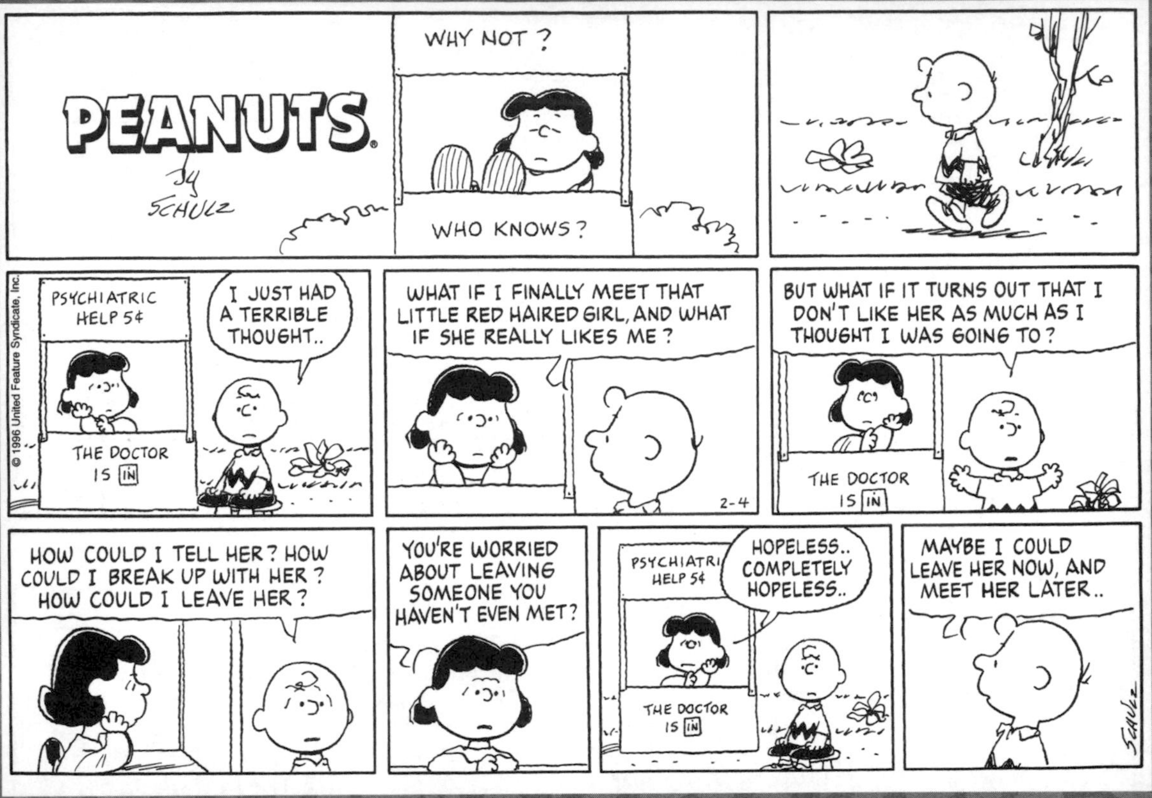
PEANUTS
SCHULZ
WHY NOT?
WHO KNOWS?
© 1996 United Feature Syndicate, Inc.
PSYCHIATRIC HELP 5¢
THE DOCTOR IS IN
I JUST HAD A TERRIBLE THOUGHT..
WHAT IF I FINALLY MEET THAT LITTLE RED HAIRED GIRL, AND WHAT IF SHE REALLY LIKES ME?
2-4
BUT WHAT IF IT TURNS OUT THAT I DON'T LIKE HER AS MUCH AS I THOUGHT I WAS GOING TO?
THE DOCTOR IS IN
HOW COULD I TELL HER? HOW COULD I BREAK UP WITH HER? HOW COULD I LEAVE HER?
YOU'RE WORRIED ABOUT LEAVING SOMEONE YOU HAVEN'T EVEN MET?
PSYCHIATRI HELP 5¢
HOPELESS.. COMPLETELY HOPELESS..
THE DOCTOR IS IN
MAYBE I COULD LEAVE HER NOW, AND MEET HER LATER..
SCHULZ

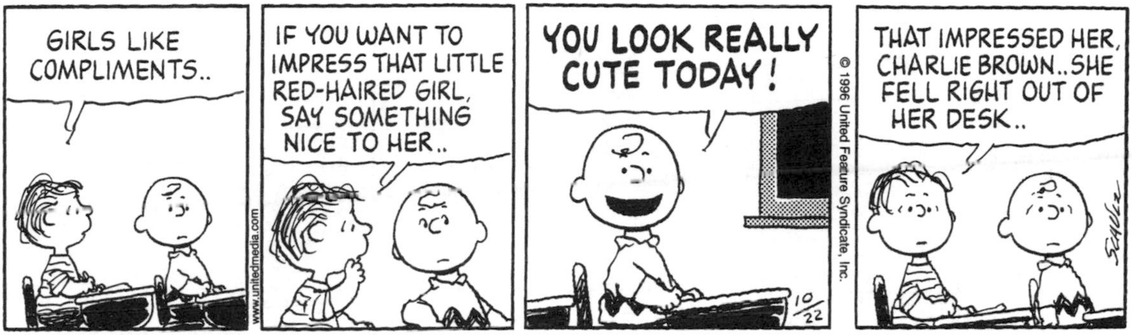
GIRLS LIKE COMPLIMENTS..
IF YOU WANT TO IMPRESS THAT LITTLE RED-HAIRED GIRL, SAY SOMETHING NICE TO HER..
YOU LOOK REALLY CUTE TODAY!
THAT IMPRESSED HER, CHARLIE BROWN.. SHE FELL RIGHT OUT OF HER DESK..
www.unitedmedia.com
© 1996 United Feature Syndicate, Inc.
10/22
SCHULZ

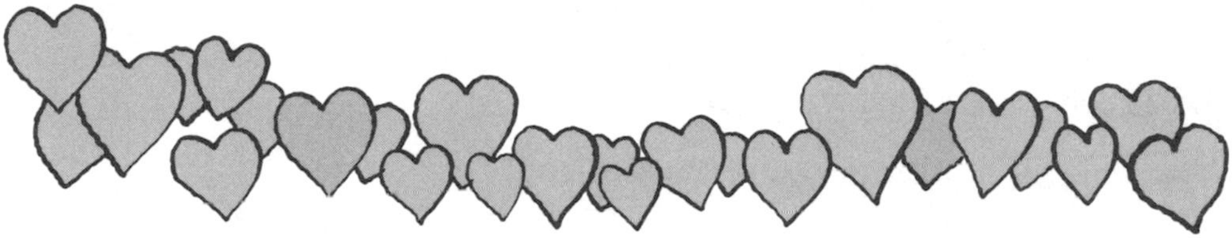

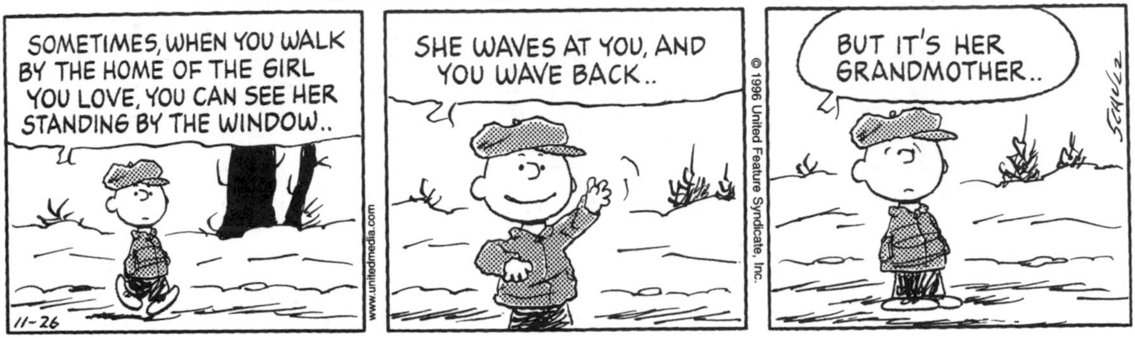
SOMETIMES, WHEN YOU WALK BY THE HOME OF THE GIRL YOU LOVE, YOU CAN SEE HER STANDING BY THE WINDOW..
11-26
www.unitedmedia.com
SHE WAVES AT YOU, AND YOU WAVE BACK..
© 1996 United Feature Syndicate, Inc.
BUT IT'S HER GRANDMOTHER..
SCHULZ

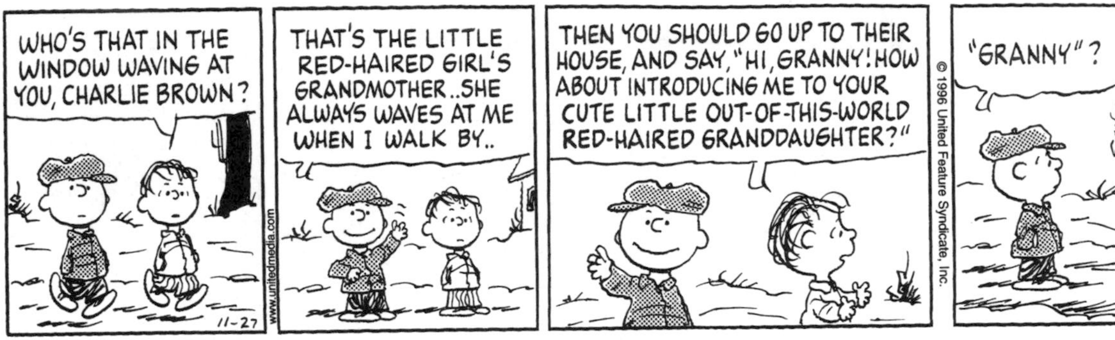
WHO'S THAT IN THE WINDOW WAVING AT YOU, CHARLIE BROWN?
11-27
www.unitedmedia.com
THAT'S THE LITTLE RED-HAIRED GIRL'S GRANDMOTHER..SHE ALWAYS WAVES AT ME WHEN I WALK BY..
THEN YOU SHOULD GO UP TO THEIR HOUSE, AND SAY, "HI, GRANNY! HOW ABOUT INTRODUCING ME TO YOUR CUTE LITTLE OUT-OF-THIS-WORLD RED-HAIRED GRANDDAUGHTER?"
© 1996 United Feature Syndicate, Inc.
"GRANNY"?
SCHULZ

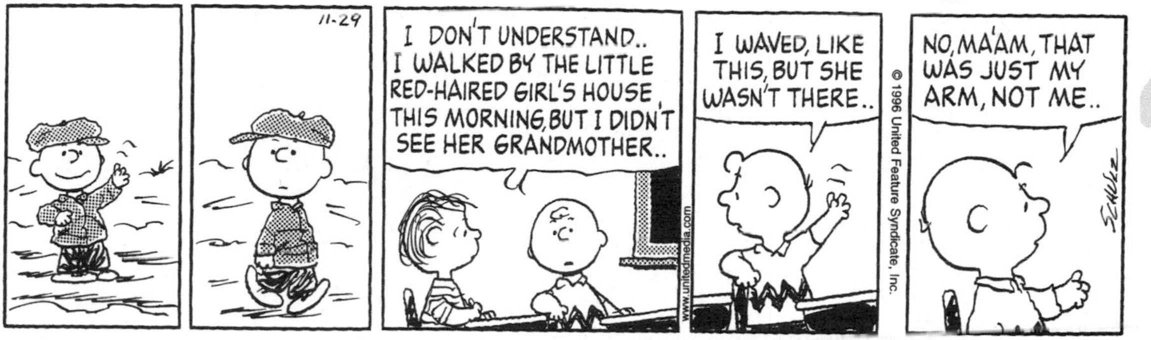
11-29
I DON'T UNDERSTAND.. I WALKED BY THE LITTLE RED-HAIRED GIRL'S HOUSE THIS MORNING, BUT I DIDN'T SEE HER GRANDMOTHER..
www.unitedmedia.com
I WAVED, LIKE THIS, BUT SHE WASN'T THERE..
© 1996 United Feature Syndicate, Inc.
NO, MA'AM, THAT WAS JUST MY ARM, NOT ME..
SCHULZ

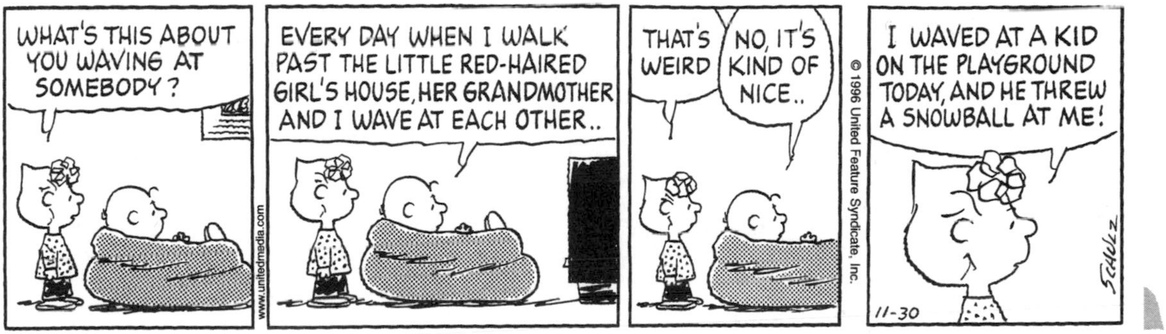
WHAT'S THIS ABOUT YOU WAVING AT SOMEBODY?
www.unitedmedia.com
EVERY DAY WHEN I WALK PAST THE LITTLE RED-HAIRED GIRL'S HOUSE, HER GRANDMOTHER AND I WAVE AT EACH OTHER..
THAT'S WEIRD
NO, IT'S KIND OF NICE..
© 1996 United Feature Syndicate, Inc.
I WAVED AT A KID ON THE PLAYGROUND TODAY, AND HE THREW A SNOWBALL AT ME!
SCHULZ
11-30

YOU KNOW WHAT I'D LIKE TO DO? I'D LIKE TO TELL YOU THAT THE LITTLE RED-HAIRED GIRL IS AT THE DOOR, AND THEN, WHEN YOU RUN TO SEE HER, I'D YELL, "APRIL FOOL!"
THAT'S WHAT I'D REALLY LIKE TO DO..
4-1
www.unitedmedia.com
BY THE WAY, THERE'S A GIANT LIZARD CRAWLING UP YOUR BACK..
AAUGH!
© 1997 United Feature Syndicate, Inc.
APRIL FOOL!
SCHULZ

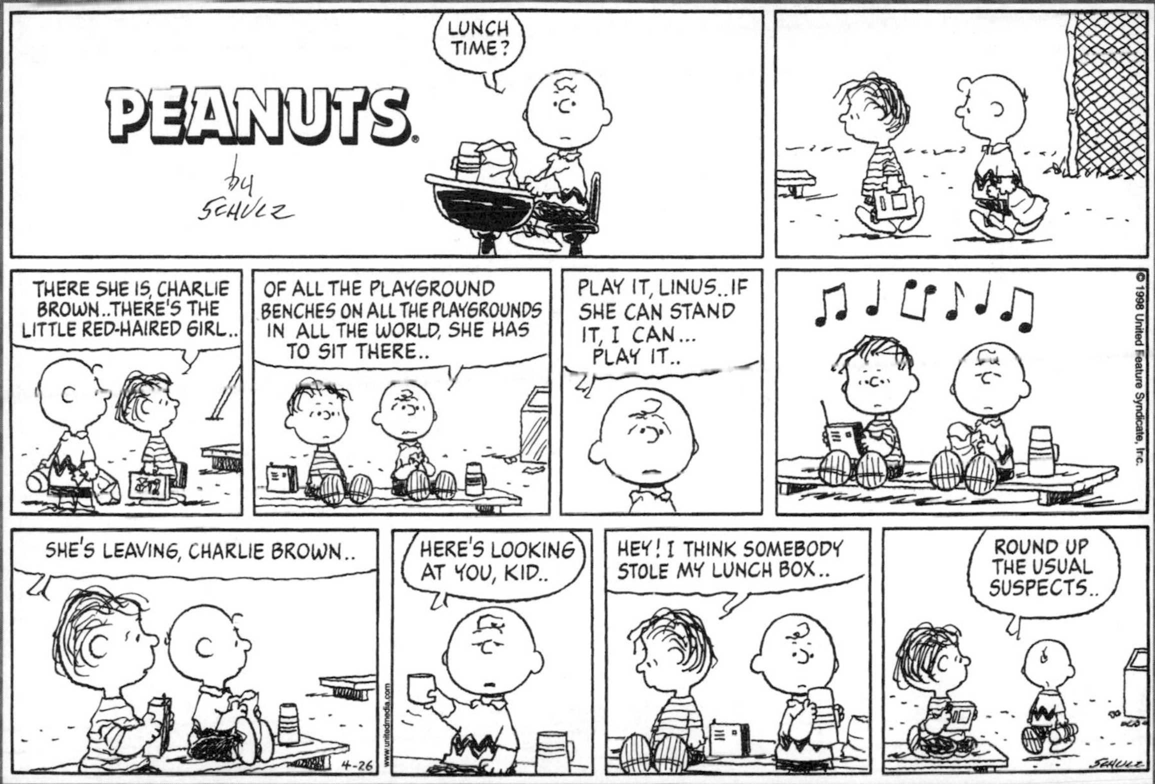
PEANUTS
by SCHULZ
LUNCH TIME?
THERE SHE IS, CHARLIE BROWN..THERE'S THE LITTLE RED-HAIRED GIRL..
OF ALL THE PLAYGROUND BENCHES ON ALL THE PLAYGROUNDS IN ALL THE WORLD, SHE HAS TO SIT THERE..
PLAY IT, LINUS..IF SHE CAN STAND IT, I CAN... PLAY IT..
© 1998 United Feature Syndicate, Inc.
SHE'S LEAVING, CHARLIE BROWN..
4-26
www.unitedmedia.com
HERE'S LOOKING AT YOU, KID..
HEY! I THINK SOMEBODY STOLE MY LUNCH BOX..
ROUND UP THE USUAL SUSPECTS..
SCHULZ

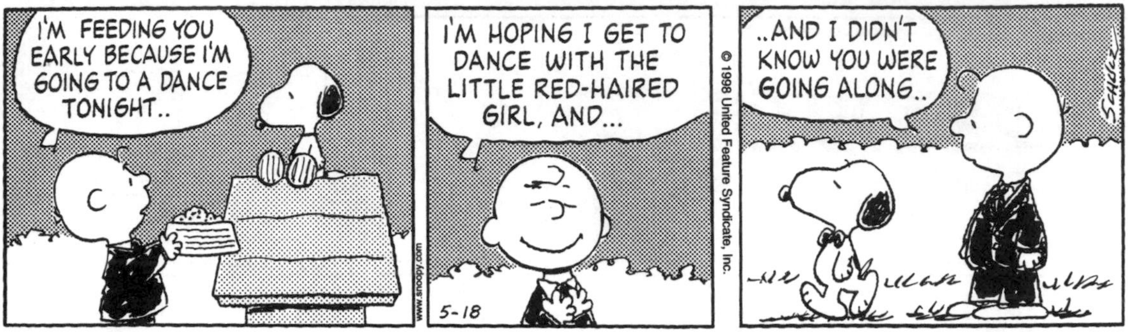

I'M FEEDING YOU EARLY BECAUSE I'M GOING TO A DANCE TONIGHT..
I'M HOPING I GET TO DANCE WITH THE LITTLE RED-HAIRED GIRL, AND...
..AND I DIDN'T KNOW YOU WERE GOING ALONG..
5-18
© 1998 United Feature Syndicate, Inc.
www.snoopy.com
SCHULZ

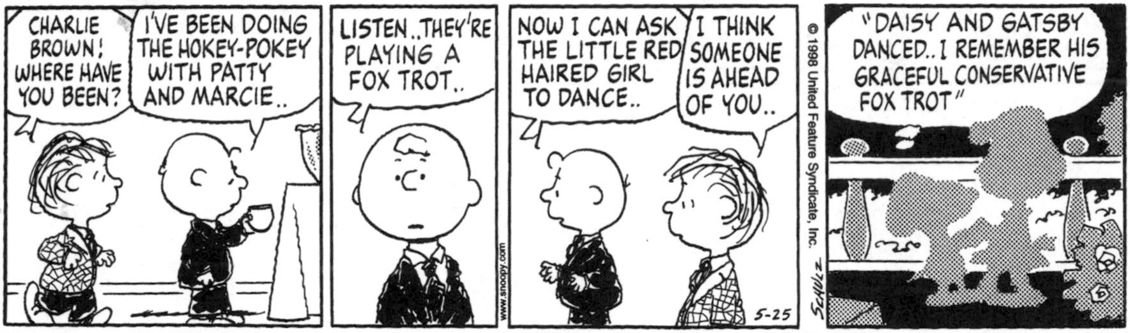

CHARLIE BROWN! WHERE HAVE YOU BEEN?
I'VE BEEN DOING THE HOKEY-POKEY WITH PATTY AND MARCIE..
LISTEN..THEY'RE PLAYING A FOX TROT..
NOW I CAN ASK THE LITTLE RED HAIRED GIRL TO DANCE..
I THINK SOMEONE IS AHEAD OF YOU..
"DAISY AND GATSBY DANCED..I REMEMBER HIS GRACEFUL CONSERVATIVE FOX TROT"
5-25
© 1998 United Feature Syndicate, Inc.
www.snoopy.com
SCHULZ

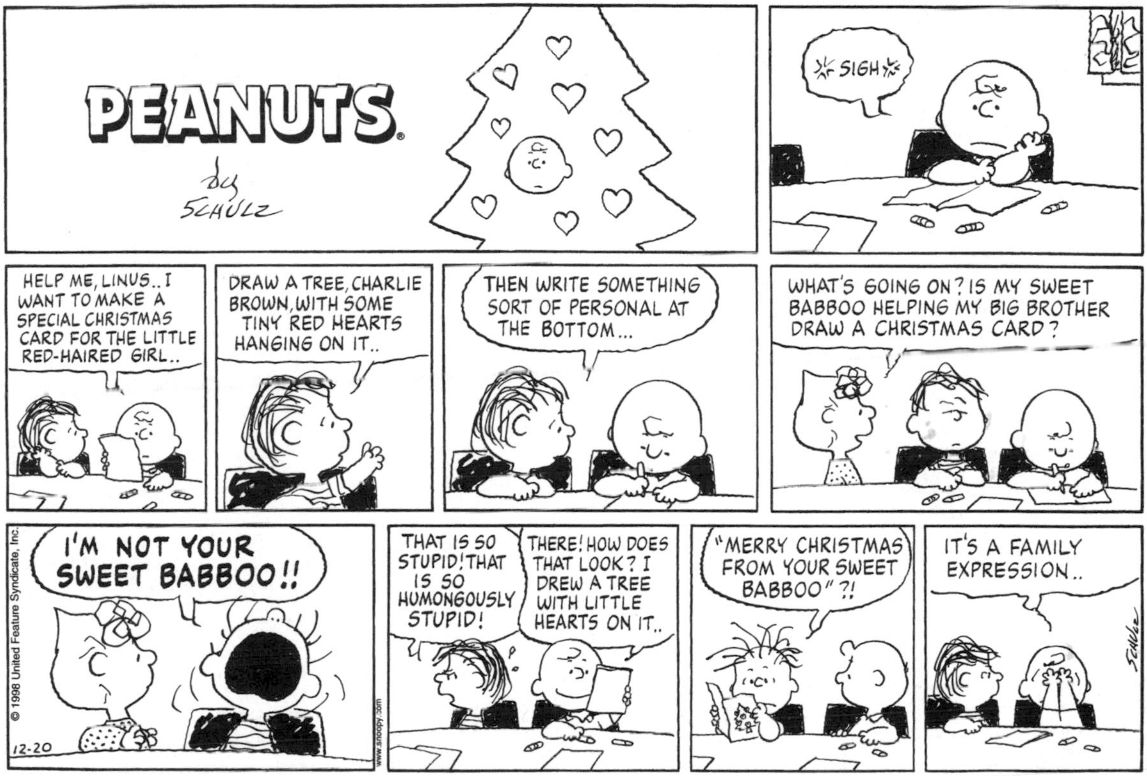
PEANUTS
by SCHULZ
SIGH
HELP ME, LINUS.. I WANT TO MAKE A SPECIAL CHRISTMAS CARD FOR THE LITTLE RED-HAIRED GIRL..
DRAW A TREE, CHARLIE BROWN, WITH SOME TINY RED HEARTS HANGING ON IT..
THEN WRITE SOMETHING SORT OF PERSONAL AT THE BOTTOM...
WHAT'S GOING ON? IS MY SWEET BABBOO HELPING MY BIG BROTHER DRAW A CHRISTMAS CARD?
I'M NOT YOUR SWEET BABBOO!!
THAT IS SO STUPID! THAT IS SO HUMONGOUSLY STUPID!
THERE! HOW DOES THAT LOOK? I DREW A TREE WITH LITTLE HEARTS ON IT..
"MERRY CHRISTMAS FROM YOUR SWEET BABBOO"?!
IT'S A FAMILY EXPRESSION..
© 1998 United Feature Syndicate, Inc.
12-20
www.snoopy.com
SCHULZ

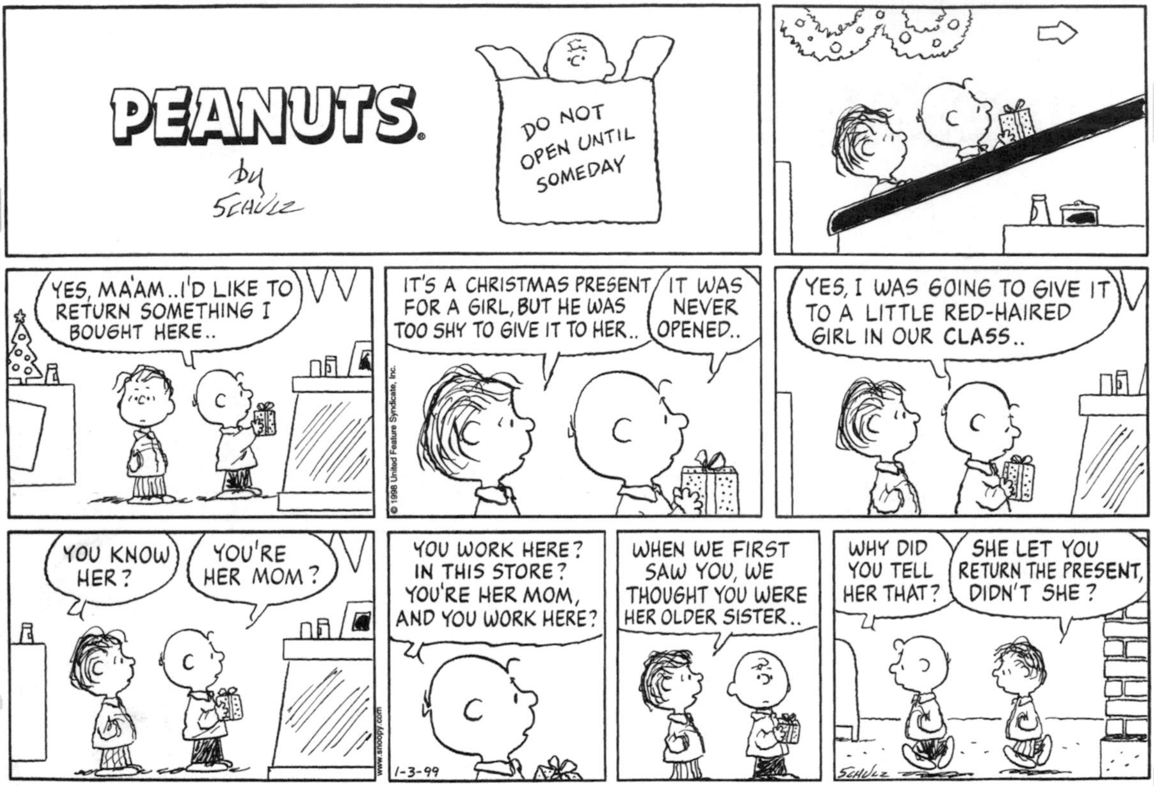
PEANUTS
by SCHULZ
DO NOT OPEN UNTIL SOMEDAY
YES, MA'AM..I'D LIKE TO RETURN SOMETHING I BOUGHT HERE..
IT'S A CHRISTMAS PRESENT FOR A GIRL, BUT HE WAS TOO SHY TO GIVE IT TO HER..
IT WAS NEVER OPENED..
YES, I WAS GOING TO GIVE IT TO A LITTLE RED-HAIRED GIRL IN OUR CLASS..
YOU KNOW HER?
YOU'RE HER MOM?
YOU WORK HERE? IN THIS STORE? YOU'RE HER MOM, AND YOU WORK HERE?
WHEN WE FIRST SAW YOU, WE THOUGHT YOU WERE HER OLDER SISTER..
WHY DID YOU TELL HER THAT?
SHE LET YOU RETURN THE PRESENT, DIDN'T SHE?
© 1998 United Feature Syndicate, Inc.
www.snoopy.com
1-3-99
SCHULZ

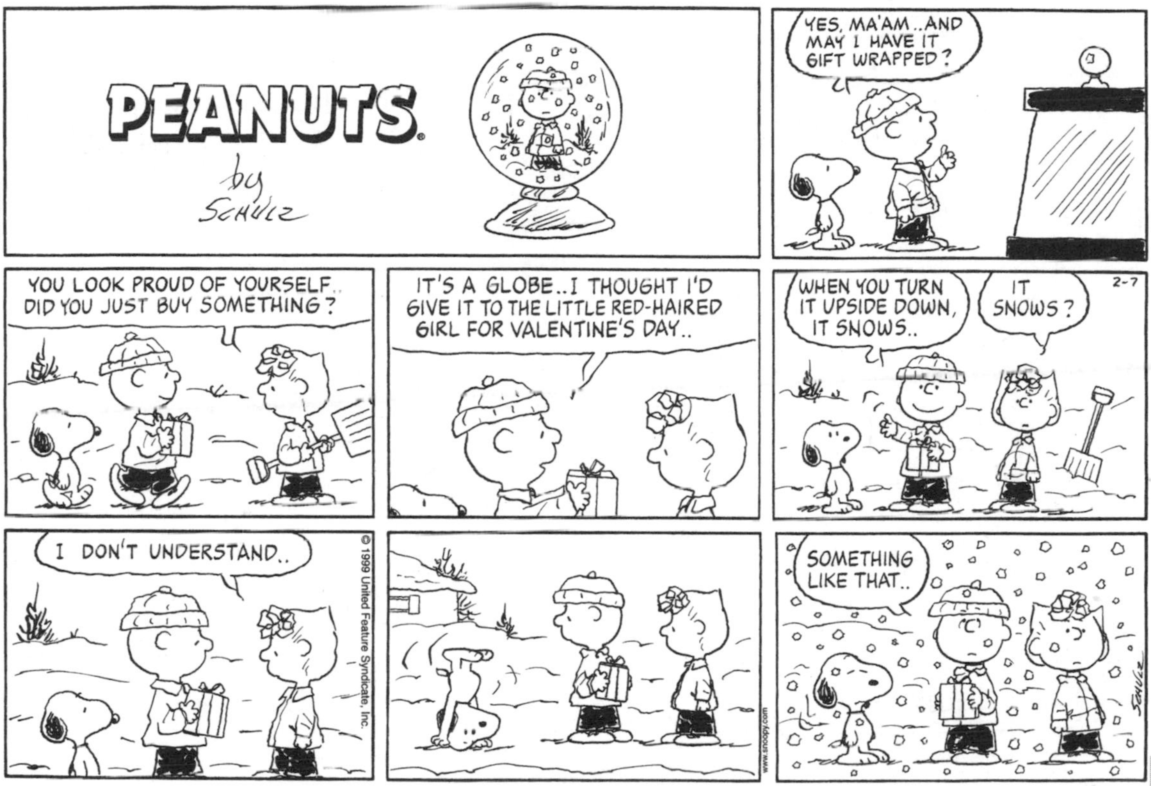
PEANUTS
by SCHULZ
YES, MA'AM..AND MAY I HAVE IT GIFT WRAPPED?
YOU LOOK PROUD OF YOURSELF.. DID YOU JUST BUY SOMETHING?
IT'S A GLOBE..I THOUGHT I'D GIVE IT TO THE LITTLE RED-HAIRED GIRL FOR VALENTINE'S DAY..
WHEN YOU TURN IT UPSIDE DOWN, IT SNOWS..
IT SNOWS?
2-7
I DON'T UNDERSTAND..
© 1999 United Feature Syndicate, Inc.
www.snoopy.com
SOMETHING LIKE THAT..
SCHULZ

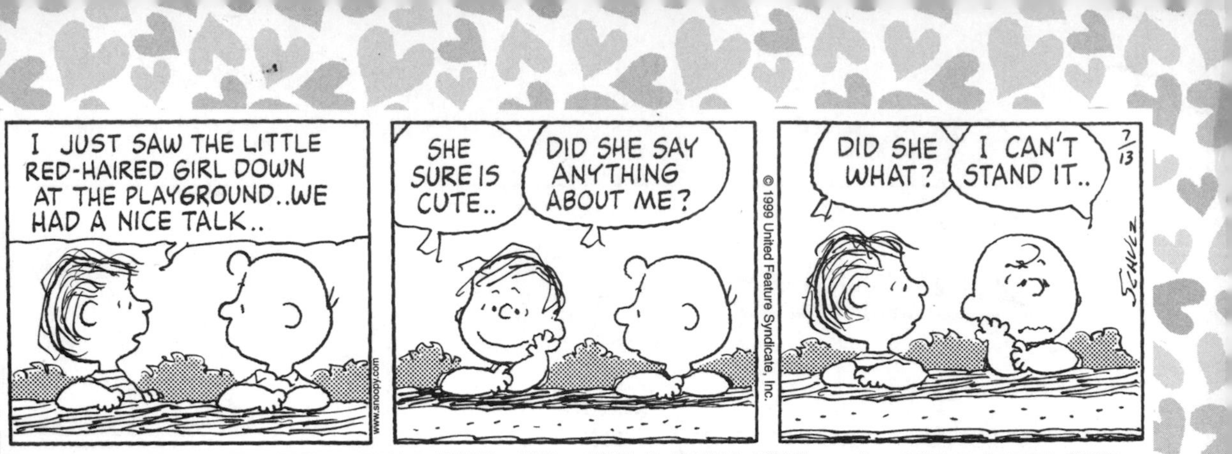
I JUST SAW THE LITTLE RED-HAIRED GIRL DOWN AT THE PLAYGROUND..WE HAD A NICE TALK..
SHE SURE IS CUTE..
DID SHE SAY ANYTHING ABOUT ME?
DID SHE WHAT?
I CAN'T STAND IT..
© 1999 United Feature Syndicate, Inc.
www.snoopy.com
7/13
SCHULZ

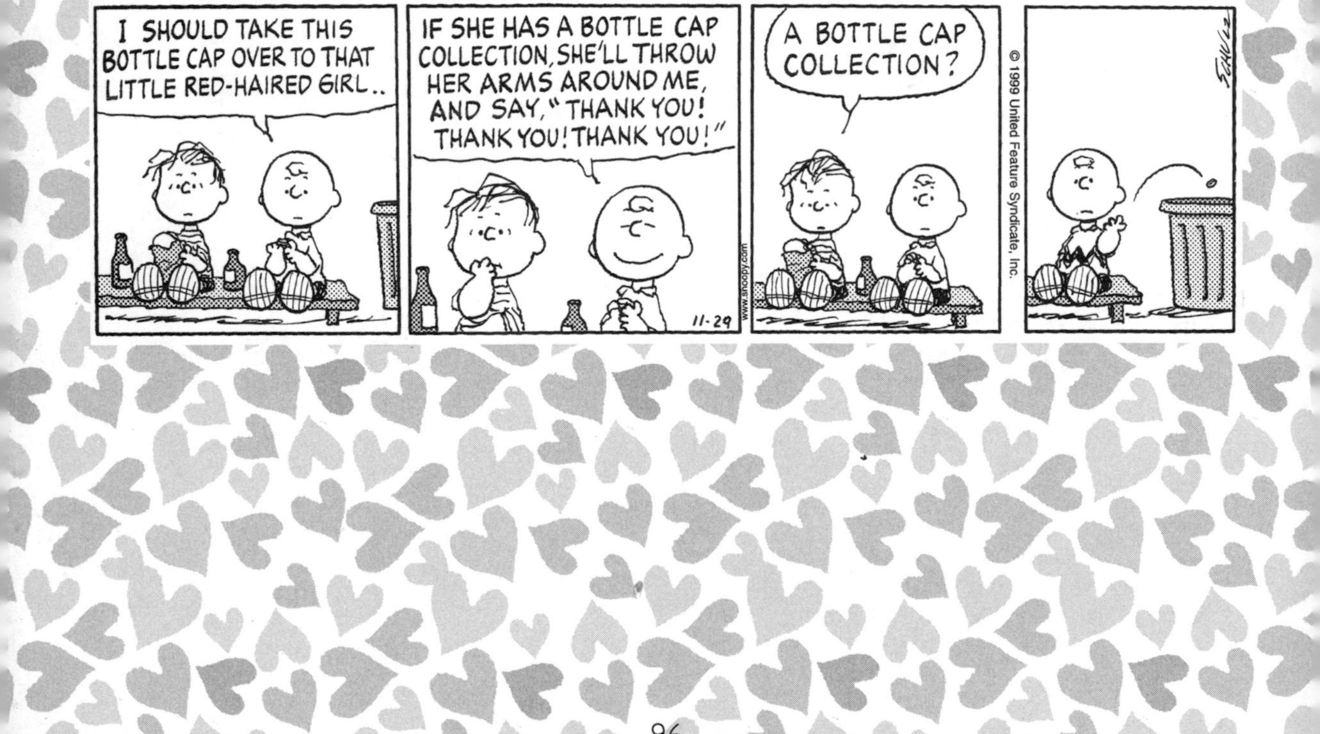
I SHOULD TAKE THIS BOTTLE CAP OVER TO THAT LITTLE RED-HAIRED GIRL..
IF SHE HAS A BOTTLE CAP COLLECTION, SHE'LL THROW HER ARMS AROUND ME, AND SAY, "THANK YOU! THANK YOU! THANK YOU!"
A BOTTLE CAP COLLECTION?
© 1999 United Feature Syndicate, Inc.
www.snoopy.com
11-29
SCHULZ